GOLDEN HARVEST

GOLDEN HARVEST

Events at the Periphery
of the Holocaust

JAN TOMASZ GROSS

WITH

IRENA GRUDZIŃSKA GROSS

OXFORD

UNIVERSITY PRESS

OXFORD
UNIVERSITY PRESS

Oxford University Press, Inc., publishes works that further
Oxford University's objective of excellence
in research, scholarship, and education.

Oxford   New York
Auckland   Cape Town   Dar es Salaam   Hong Kong   Karachi
Kuala Lumpur   Madrid   Melbourne   Mexico City   Nairobi
New Delhi   Shanghai   Taipei   Toronto

With offices in
Argentina   Austria   Brazil   Chile   Czech Republic   France   Greece
Guatemala   Hungary   Italy   Japan   Poland   Portugal   Singapore
South Korea   Switzerland   Thailand   Turkey   Ukraine   Vietnam

Copyright © 2012 by Jan Tomasz Gross and Irena Grudzińska Gross

Published by Oxford University Press, Inc.
198 Madison Avenue, New York, New York 10016

www.oup.com

Oxford is a registered trademark of Oxford University Press

ISBN-13: 9780199731671

Photograph courtesy of Muzeum Walki i Męczeństwa Treblinka.
Copyright: Agencja Gazeta

1 3 5 7 9 8 6 4 2

Printed in the United States of America
on acid-free paper

A golden tooth ripped from a corpse will be always bleeding.

Kazimierz Wyka, *Życie na niby* (As if life)

CONTENTS

CONTENTS

x

CONTENTS

INTRODUCTION

The inspiration for this book came from a photograph published for the first time in *Gazeta Wyborcza*, the largest Polish daily, on January 8, 2008. The photograph appeared as an illustration to an article by Piotr Głuchowski and Marcin Kowalski about the postwar practice of digging through mass graves at the site of the Treblinka extermination camp.[1] Gleaners, or, as they were called at the time, "diggers" (*kopacze*), sifted through the ashes and remains of murdered Jews at sites of all the Nazi extermination camps in Poland (Treblinka, Bełżec, Sobibór, Chełmno, and Auschwitz) for many years after the war, looking for pieces of jewelry and dental gold overlooked by the Nazis. Occasionally local police would chase them away.

Głuchowski and Kowalski received this photograph from Tadeusz Kiryluk, an inhabitant of the village Wólka Okrąglik, adjacent to the Treblinka camp. Kiryluk was a former director of the Museum in Treblinka. The photograph, he explained, shows a group of local peasants caught by the police shortly after the war, while digging at Treblinka.[2]

---

[1] Marcin Kowalski and Piotr Głuchowski, "Gorączka złota w Treblince" (Gold fever in Treblinka), *Gazeta Wyborcza*, January 8, 2008.

[2] Marcin Kowalski and Piotr Głuchowski, "Kto jest na tym zdjęciu" (Who is in this photograph), *Gazeta Wyborcza*, January 26, 2011; see also editorial note in *Gazeta Wyborcza* on March 14, 2011.

I was stunned by the power of the scene caught in the photograph, and equally stunned that no one had noticed the picture upon its publication. My book *Fear: Anti-Semitism in Poland after Auschwitz* came out in Polish the same month, triggering a wide-ranging discussion in the media about Polish-Jewish relations after the war.[3] I was swept up in it, and the photograph slipped away from my mind. But when Oxford University Press invited me a year later to write a small book drawing on a single photograph iconic in my field of study, I immediately thought about it again.

Even before *Golden Harvest* appeared in Poland, the photograph became a source of controversy. An early draft of the book began to circulate on the Internet, and two journalists from the daily *Rzeczpospolita* researched the origin of the photograph, trying to prove that it was not from Treblinka and did not show diggers. Another effort to discredit the photograph was attempted by Marcin Kącki in *Gazeta Wyborcza*.[4] Once the book was published in Poland and the general public became acquainted with its subject—the collusion of the Polish population in the pillaging and killing of Jews at the periphery of the Holocaust—journalists' preoccupation with the photograph served as a distraction, to avoid discussion of what the book was really about.[5]

---

[3] *Fear: Anti-Semitism in Poland after Auschwitz. An Essay in Historical Interpretation* (New York: Random House, 2006); and *Strach: Antysemityzm w Polsce tuż po wojnie. Historia moralnej zapaści* (Kraków: Znak, 2008). Kowalski and Głuchowski wrote their article inspired by the publication of *Fear*.

[4] Michał Majewski and Paweł Reszka, "Tajemnice starej fotografii" (Secrets of an old photograph), *Rzeczpospolita*, January 22–23, 2011; Marcin Kącki, "Powiększenie: Nowe oblicze znanego zdjęcia" (Enlargement: New aspects of an old photograph), *Gazeta Wyborcza*, March 18, 2011.

[5] On the collusion, see "The Peripheries of the Holocaust" chapter.
See Jan T. Gross and Irena Grudzińska Gross, "Zamieszanie wokół zdjęcia" (Confusion concerning the photograph), *Gazeta Wyborcza*, March 26, 2011.

While working on the book I discussed it frequently with Irena Grudzińska Gross. We decided that Irena should write down her observations and that we would cowrite the book. We had published two volumes of wartime documents in the past,[6] so *Golden Harvest* would be a sort of reprise of our former collaboration. We would like to express our gratitude to a number of friends and colleagues who read early versions of the manuscript and offered suggestions and assistance. Our thanks go in particular to Anna Bikont, Roman and Halina Frydman, Jan Grabowski, Robert Kuwałek, Marcel Łoziński, Scott Moyers, Jonathan Schell, Alina Skibińska, Joanna Szczęsna, Joanna Tokarska-Bakir, Wojciech Wołyński, our editor at Znak, Maciej Gablankowski, and our editor at Oxford University Press, Timothy Bent.

The Polish-language edition of *Golden Harvest* came out in March 2011. We are grateful to Znak, our publisher, for standing up to various attempts at intimidation, including an email campaign to jam Internet addresses of its editorial offices.

During our book promotion tour in Poland we were invited to a news analysis program on the main channel of Polish television, *Mam inne zdanie* (I have a different opinion, March 15, 2011). Several people were assembled for an hour-long discussion about *Golden Harvest*, including the two journalists from *Rzeczpospolita*. After the program a young man who was sitting in the audience came up to us and asked, "Tell me, please, what is your book about?"

[6] Jan T. Gross and Irena Grudzińska-Gross, eds., *War through Children's Eyes* (Stanford, Calif.: Hoover Institution Press, 1981); Jan T. Gross and Irena Grudzińska-Gross, *"W czterdziestym nas matko na Sibir zesłali . . ."* (We were sent to Siberia, Mother, in nineteen forty) (London: Aneks, 1983).

GOLDEN HARVEST

THE PHOTOGRAPH

IT IS A FAMILIAR IMAGE, ONE PEOPLE HAVE SEEN IN COUNTLESS variations: a group of peasants at harvest time after work, resting contentedly with their tools behind a pile of crops. Some may have taken a snapshot of this kind on summer vacations, while visiting distant relatives in the countryside; others might carry it as a souvenir of their days as a student volunteer, when they helped farmers in the backcountry. It is the kind of image that was featured every summer on the front pages of newspapers in communist countries half the world over, and visitors can find more or less artistically refined renditions in art galleries and museums.

Yet despite the bucolic setting, this particular photograph is disquieting—and not just because it's out of focus. Something feels off-kilter about the landscape, which cannot be pegged easily to a geographical location. Were palm trees rather than conifers protruding from behind the group one might place the setting of the photograph in a desert. The image seems familiar and strange at the same time. And when one notes what is scattered in front of the group the mystery deepens: skulls and bones.

Where are we? Who are the people in the photograph?

We are in the middle of Europe right after World War II. The peasants in the photograph are standing atop a mountain of ashes. These are the ashes of 800,000 Jews gassed and cremated in the Treblinka extermination camp between July 1942 and October 1943. The peasants have been digging through remains of Holocaust victims, hoping to find gold and precious stones that their Nazi executioners overlooked.

This innocent-looking image links two central events of the Holocaust: the mass murder of European Jews and the accompanying looting of their property. For proof of an indissoluble bond between these two activities we need only to listen to an exchange that took place in the *anus mundi*, the gas chamber at Auschwitz, between a prisoner, Filip Muller, who had just been brought there to work in the Sonderkommando—"work units," composed of Jewish prisoners forced to help dispose of the bodies— and an SS guard. After a transport of Slovak Jews was gassed in the spring of 1942, Sonderkommando prisoners were ordered to strip the bodies. "Before me lay the corpse of a woman. With trembling hands and shaking all over I began to remove her stockings. It was the first time in my life that I had touched a dead body. She was not yet quite cold. As I pulled the stocking down her leg, it tore." An SS solider named Stark, who had been watching, struck Muller, bellowing, "What the hell d'you think you're doing? Pay attention, and get a move on! These things are to be used again."[1]

Franz Stangl, the first commander of the Sobibór extermination camp and subsequently reassigned to Treblinka, was asked, when in jail after the war, by the British journalist Gitta Sereny why he thought the Jews were being exterminated. "They wanted their money," he immediately replied. "Have you any idea of the fantastic sums that were involved?" The profitability of the whole enterprise was, it seems, high on the agenda of the perpetrators. The SS leader and police chief in Lublin, Odilo Globocnik, who was in charge of "Operation

[1] Filip Muller, *Eyewitness Auschwitz: Three Years in the Gas Chambers* (Chicago: Ivan R. Dee, 1999), 12.

Reinhard,"[2] ordered Stangl to Treblinka in the middle of August 1942. "We've already sent a hundred thousand Jews up there and nothing has arrived here in money or materials." Globocnik wanted Stangl to find out what was happening to their property.[3]

Stangl acquitted himself very well in this assignment. Soon transports began to leave from Treblinka—over a thousand freight cars, filled with the belongings of murdered Jews. In addition to money and jewelry, the SS dispatched goods accompanied by shipment lists, which were checked by railroad employees at the Treblinka train station. Hence the detailed knowledge of Franciszek Ząbecki, a train dispatcher there:

> Into freight-cars separately male coats tied in bundles were loaded, separately, men's suits, jackets, trousers; again separately, children's clothing and women's wardrobe—dresses, blouses, sweaters, old and new, caps, hats; separately, men's tall boots, and male, female and children's shoes. Men's, women's, and children's underwear, separately, used and new items, swaddle cloths, pillows, cushions . . . suitcases filled with pencils, fountain pens, and glasses, umbrellas and canes tied in separate bundles. They also shipped spools of thread of all kinds and colors. Leather for the production of shoes was tied in separate bundles, hard sheets for manufacture of soles, leather for

[2] The program of murdering all the Jews in occupied Poland (or, as it was called then, in the Generalgouvernement) was named in honor of Reinhard Heydrich, the head of the Reich's Main Security Office and the protector of Bohemia and Moravia assassinated by the Czech underground.

[3] Gitta Sereny, *Into That Darkness: From Mercy Killing to Mass Murder* (New York: McGraw Hill, 1974), 101, 133.

THE PHOTOGRAPH

bags, clothes. In cardboard boxes shaving utensils were packed, razors, hair-cutting clippers, mirrors, even pots and pans, washbasins, carpentry tools, saws, planes, hammers, in general everything that could be brought over by several hundred thousand people. . . . They also shipped shaved women's hair. The load was described as a military cargo: *Gut der Waffen SS* [Property of Waffen SS]. Freight cars were dispatched to Germany and sometimes to SS-Arbeitslager in Lublin.[4]

Lublin was where Globocnik and the staff of Operation Reinhard were stationed.

Globocnik was the fox guarding the chicken coop. He had been *Gauleiter*—political leader of a district under Nazi control—in Vienna, but got fired for corruption. The fleecing of Vienna Jews carried out after the Anschluss (the incorporation of Austria into the Reich in 1938) was an exemplary case of "Aryanization"—in other words, the confiscation of Jewish property—in which one Adolf Eichmann showed his mettle for the first time. As the top party official in Vienna, Globocnik eagerly gave Eichmann a helping hand—a trifle too eagerly, it seems. Becoming SS and police chief in the Lublin district was his second chance to build a career in the Nazi hierarchy. A few years later both Eichmann and Globocnik would emerge as key figures in the implementation of the Nazis' "final solution of the Jewish question." Heinrich Himmler, the commander of the German police and the SS, was particularly fond of Globocnik. "My dear Globus," he wrote, using a nickname in official correspondence, "I got your letter of

---

[4] Franciszek Ząbecki, *Wspomnienia dawne i nowe* (Old and new recollections) (Warsaw: Instytut Wydawniczy PAX, 1977), 73.

November 4, 1943, with the final report on the 'Operation Reinhard.'"[5]

THE NEED TO NAME

Operation Reinhard's objective was the total annihilation of the three million Jews inhabiting the Generalgouvernement—the part of Poland under Nazi control. How to describe such an undertaking? Any generation that did not experience the Holocaust can learn about it only from words, and the knowledge thus gained is never complete. The right words, however, are difficult to find. People who perished had no voice, and those who survived were pushed into a realm of silence by the singular character of their experiences. The violence they had endured—in concentration camps, in hiding, or in prisons—destroyed their capacity for making contact with the world. Their experience was and remains in great measure inexpressible, because pain and physical violence destroy language and cause a reversion to a state anterior to language.[6] Still, trauma demands to be expressed. What is horrific remains horrific so long as it is not named. Once a name is attached to it, the horror retreats; it diminishes, since the very act of naming

---

[5] Thomas Blatt, *Sobibor: The Forgotten Revolt. A Survivor's Report* (Issaquah, Wa., H.E.P., 1997), 92.

[6] Elaine Scarry, *The Body in Pain* (Oxford: Oxford University Press, 1985).

reconnects the victim to the world. Theodor Adorno wrote that what the Nazis did to the Jews was inexpressible. Yet a way of expressing it must be found if we do not want to doom the victims to oblivion. Their number was too great to name them one by one. This is why, Adorno believed, the concept of "genocide" was invented.[7] That term acknowledged the facts, codified and inscribed what was inexpressible into the international declaration of human rights, normalizing it and rendering it measurable. But the codification did not render "what the Nazis did to the Jews" easier to express.[8]

Adorno was confirming the need for naming the Shoah in a public, institutional language: a crime requires legal codification. Other writers and thinkers have demanded different sorts of naming, of revealing and remembering of these events. Paul Celan remarked that naming returns what has happened to the living. But in public discourse—in the articles of historians and journalists— euphemisms are often used to talk about extremes of violence. Such euphemisms play, to use Joanna Tokarska-Bakir's formulation, a "side-stepping role."

In private life as well we have difficulties talking about genocide. When we encounter descriptions of extermination, whatever our temporal distance, our first reaction is to push that knowledge away. Our memory keeps that knowledge in some distant and dark corner, and moves a different history into the forefront: the history of human heroism, of solidarity. The Shoah reminds us not only of

[7] "Genocide" is a term created by Rafael Lemkin (1900–1959), a Polish lawyer of Jewish descent who lost most of his family during the war. He was one of the authors of the Convention on the Prevention and Punishment of the Crime of Genocide, which was adopted by the United Nations on December 9, 1948.

[8] Theodor W. Adorno, fragment III of the appendix for *Minima Moralia*, vol. 4, in *Gesammelte Schriften in Zwanzig Bänden* (Frankfurt am Main: Suhrkamp, 1951).

death but also of human bestiality. Yet human bestiality is taboo. This is one of the reasons for the constant return to the theme of the inexpressibility of the Shoah: speaking about it is always awkward; the moment for it is never right, the tone never proper. The topic is so scorching that touching it can only burn.

The Treblinka photograph does not seem at first to refer to any of this. It is reminiscent of harvest iconography—not quite a celebration, but a restful pause. The whiteness of the women's headscarves and the men's shirts, the sunlight, the ground as if ploughed. A good photograph, according to Susan Sontag, "is like a quotation, or a maxim or proverb."[9] It catches a certain reality and transmits it to us instantaneously. In this sense, the photograph is not good, because its meaning is not easily caught. It needs to be examined, interpreted. What is important—bones, skulls—though in the foreground, seem to be hidden, unclear. The feelings and thoughts of the people sitting around them are also inscrutable. We do not know who the photographer was or what his purpose was in taking the picture. Judging by its quality, he was not a professional, and this adds authenticity to the photo, a documentary character. Judging by the uniforms and weapons, we are in the mid-1940s. Some time has already passed since the closing of the death camp; the skulls and bones have been bleached white.

The situation depicted in the photo is semi-official: the peasants, most probably inhabitants of the environs of Treblinka, are surrounded by soldiers or militiamen, but there is no visible tension between the two groups. Those in uniform stand close to the civilians. People are busy positioning themselves for the camera, pushing

---

[9] Susan Sontag, *Regarding the Pain of Others* (New York: Farrar, Straus and Giroux, 2003), 22.

against their neighbors, talking to each other. The bones and skulls have been placed in an orderly display in front of the assembled. Nobody is looking at them. Something seems to be happening in the middle of the group: more people are turned in that direction than looking at the photographer. Perhaps they are still arranging themselves for the photo. Their gestures and interaction underline the normalcy of their situation, preparing to pose or just chatting. This scene must have been accompanied by a lot of noise (and the stench of rotting bodies). It is as if they have gathered for a reunion after a productive day of work: rather calm, just tired.

Unlike in so many pictures of our day, nobody is smiling for the camera. The subjects are serious, diffident. They were likely not accustomed to being photographed. Perhaps they were even worried about the photo's future use. It could be used as proof of their presence in that place of profanation. But they quite spontaneously form a semicircle, as for traditional group photos, for example, those taken of peasants after harvest. In this case the harvest was Jewish gold and valuables. One could imagine that if this photo were reproduced in newspapers, its caption would probably be something like "After a Day's Work."

TAKING OVER JEWISH PROPERTY

The phenomenon that has been captured in the photograph— the plundering of Jewish property, in this case gold fillings and jewelry—started in Nazi-conquered Europe long before the

Holocaust. Associating Jews with money or with gold, in addition to imagining them as God-killers, is one of the most prevalent anti-Semitic clichés. Both phantasmagorias share a common trope, that of the Jew as a bloodsucker. Metaphorically this applies equally to the Jew as a ritual murderer and to the Jew perceived as an exploiter.

Alongside tales of Jewish conspiracies—a "fifth column," allegedly delivering a stab in the back, sowing subversion as "Judeo-Bolsheviks"—anti-Semitic propaganda always demanded elimination of Jews from the national economy (as well as barring them from state employment) in order to liberate subjugated peoples from alleged Jewish enslavement.[10] The plunder of Jewish wealth started years before Jews had been turned into ashes in Nazi extermination camps. German, Austrian, and Czechoslovakian Jewry fell victim to the process of Aryanization even prior to the outbreak of war.

"'Aryanization' of Jewish assets under National-Socialist rule was one of the most prodigious property-transfers in modern times."[11] It proceeded along two main tracks: the issuance of laws imposing on Jews the obligation to surrender ownership of their assets (i.e., Aryanization proper) and taxation, fees, and foreign-currency exchange laws connected to the forced emigration policy to which Jews were subjected in the Third Reich. Adolf Eichmann

[10] Modern-day conspiracy theories feed off a fake produced in 1903 by the tsarist secret police, *The Protocols of the Elders of Zion*. It purports to document an alleged Jewish conspiracy to rule the world. See, for example, Binjamin W. Segel, *A Lie and a Libel: The History of the Protocols of the Elders of Zion* (Lincoln: University of Nebraska Press, 1995).

[11] Frank Bajohr, "The Beneficiaries of 'Aryanization': Hamburg as a Case Study," *Yad Vashem Studies* 26 (1998).

turned out to be one of the most effective bureaucrats in this domain. Drawing on the experience he gained from it, he later organized a highly efficient system of shipping Jews to extermination camps.

With the passage of time, rules and policies governing the property of Jewish émigrés became increasingly stringent and confiscatory. By the end of 1938 Jews who had not felt compelled to emigrate earlier (for many, Kristallnacht was the final warning signal) could take along but a minuscule portion of their wealth.

In addition to benefiting the state treasury, as well as those individuals who directly obtained ownership titles, Aryanization also served as a source of patronage for the Nazi Party. It allowed Gauleiters to fill party coffers and reward party faithful in their districts. Jewish assets also lined the pockets of a host of intermediaries—bankers, realtors, lawyers, civil servants—who facilitated those transactions. In the conclusion of his fine study on the beneficiaries of Aryanization in Hamburg, Frank Bajohr makes a point that applies generally to all European territories occupied by the Third Reich: "Even if it was the National Socialist state which extracted the greatest financial benefit from Aryanization, no other measure of Nazi Jewish policy ultimately involved so many actors, and above all, so many profiteers."[12]

The aspect of Aryanization directly relevant to the photograph was the taking over of precious metals owned by the Jews. Following a series of confiscatory measures passed in March 1939, the Reich government ordered Jews to surrender

[12] Bajohr, "The Beneficiaries of 'Aryanization.'"

gold, silver, and platinum to state-run pawnshops. Appraising their value at a low rate provided ample opportunity to fleece rightful owners.[13]

Only a few years later extermination camp victims' valuables would be pillaged by Nazi officials. They would be deposited at "the German National Bank by SS-Hauptsturmfuhrer Bruno Melmer on seventy six occasions between August 1942 and the end of 1944. These shipments consisted of valuables and dental work taken from deportees or their corpses."[14] In addition, precious metals plundered from Eastern European ghettos were independently sent to the Reich.[15] A former intern in the Reinickendorf smeltery recalled, "the crowns and the bridges, there were those where the teeth were still attached. . . . That was the most depressing, the fact that everything was still there. It was probably just like it had been when broken out of a mouth. The teeth were

---

[13] Beyond their monetary value as convertible currency to finance purchases abroad, precious metals were necessary to sustain important sectors of weapons-related production. "German domestic economy never experienced a serious shortage of precious metals after the first year of fighting." Almost all of the gold acquired by the German National Bank during the war was plundered, predominantly from the vaults of national banks of occupied European countries. According to the best estimates available, "only" some 15 percent of the loot came from private persons or firms. Peter Hayes, *From Cooperation to Complicity: Degussa in the Third Reich* (Cambridge, U.K.: Cambridge University Press, 2004), 169, 175, 188.

[14] Swiss creditors were paid by the German National Bank with at least 119.5 kilograms of Melmer gold (Hayes, *From Cooperation to Complicity*, 181, 183).

[15] "To take one illustration, in July 1942, just before Bruno Melmer began his visits to the National Bank, the Warsaw Office of the SS informed Heinrich Himmler that two metric tons of gold, presumably extorted from the ghetto in that city and its environs, already had been sent to Lublin and another 629 kilograms collected" (Hayes, *From Cooperation to Complicity*, 184).

still there and sometimes still bloody and with pieces of gums on them."[16]

In yet another indication that "Jewish gold" and death were somehow symbiotic, Degussa, the industrial concern that played a leading role in the processing, refinement, and trading abroad of the "Jew metals" on behalf of the Reich treasury, also manufactured at its subsidiary the disinfectant prussic acid, known as Zyklon-B, used to murder close to a million Jews in the gas chambers of Auschwitz.

Hitler's anti-Jewish obsession cannot, of course, be reduced simply to a desire to take Jewish property, although as these examples show, he appreciated the benefits that resulted. Soon after Clemens Krauss, an artist whose work Hitler fancied, took over the directorship of the Bavarian State Opera in the spring of 1942, the head of the Nazi Party's chancellery, Martin Bormann, sent the following letter to the mayor of Munich: "Today I reported to the Führer about the correspondence from the general director Krauss. The Führer wished you to check one more time to see whether a few more Jewish apartments could be made available for the newly contracted members of the Bavarian State Opera." While a Nazi "Old Fighter" (Alte Kämpfer, referring to the earliest members of the Party), Alfred Rosenberg, who in one of his capacities—leader of the so-called *Einsatzstab* Rosenberg—supervised the plunder of Jewish property in Europe, wrote to Hitler in April 1943: "My Führer, with the wish to make you happy for your birthday, I allow myself to submit to

---

[16] ARD, "Report," October 12, 1998, Eric Fielder and Oliver Merz, "Zeugen des Grauens—Teil 2: Der SS-Buchhalter Melmer," quoted in Hayes, *From Cooperation to Complicity*, 193.

you a folder with photos of some of the most valuable paintings from Jewish ownerless property secured by my Commando in the occupied western territories. . . . This folder gives but a weak impression of the extraordinary value and quantity of the art objects seized by my agency in France and put in security in the Reich."[17]

Of course, Nazi anti-Semitism also worked at a higher plane than mere economics; it rested on a conspiratorial vision of history and contempt rooted in a version of social Darwinism. And when principles guaranteeing equality before the law were abolished, the practices of state institutions, sanctioning discrimination against and gradual expropriation of Jews, as well as their removal from state employment, opened the way for social mobility and material improvement to everybody else.

This process takes different forms in the Third Reich and in the countries occupied by or allied with Germany. Its evolution in Poland was different from that in France, Hungary, or Greece. But from the standpoint of local societies, state anti-Semitism (whether indigenous or introduced by an occupying power) has this advantage: it allows for the takeover and redistribution of Jewish property among non-Jews.

Occupied Europe experienced two kinds of exploitation simultaneously. The Nazis appropriated the resources of and victimized each defeated country. But in addition they targeted and were particularly harsh toward the Jews. And this aspect of their policies usually met with a lesser or greater degree of support among the rest of the conquered populations. In Poland "a large segment" or

---

[17] Saul Friedlander, *The Years of Extermination: Nazi Germany and the Jews, 1939–1945* (New York: HarperCollins, 2007), 369, 481.

"broad stratum" of society was, in the words of Jan Karski, an eminent figure in the Polish resistance, pleased with the initial German policies directed against the Jews.[18] In Germany itself "throughout the twelve years of the Third Reich," writes Saul Friedlander, "looting of Jewish property was of the essence. It was the most easily understood and most widely adhered-to aspect of the anti-Jewish campaign, rationalized, if necessary, by the simplest ideological tenets."[19]

Nazi radicalism notwithstanding, public opinion in Europe was well conditioned to accept discrimination against the Jews. In France, for example, about half of the political parties put forth anti-Semitic slogans before the war. In prewar Poland, Hungary, and Romania, political anti-Semitism was even more entrenched. Complemented by the obscurantist anti-Semitism of Christian churches and the moral authority they wielded with their constituencies, it is hardly surprising that elimination of Jews from economic life was welcomed both by elites and the general public all across the European continent.

To achieve social standing and material comfort through one's own efforts is difficult and time-consuming. It is much easier to take over the wealth accumulated by somebody else—a particularly appealing alternative, if it can be accomplished with the blessing of the law.

---

[18] David Engel, "An Early Account of Polish Jewry under Nazi and Soviet Occupation Presented to the Polish Government-in-Exile, February 1940," *Jewish Social Studies* 45, no. 1 (1983).

[19] Friedlander, *The Years of Extermination*, 497.

PHOTOGRAPHS AND
DOCUMENTATION OF THE SHOAH

A photograph, according to a well-known saying, is worth a thousand words, yet the knowledge that it imparts is, strictly speaking, unique: the recording of a fraction of a second after the camera's lens shutter has been opened. What, then, allows us to consider such a narrowly confined piece of information as offering insight into the nature of things, or the general state of affairs, as we often do? Are we succumbing to an illusion? And yet it is by looking at a photograph, say, of Hitler at the receiving stand of a Nuremberg party rally, or of naked people being shot by SS men over a ditch, that we consolidate a significant *general* understanding about the nature of National Socialism.

What underlies that understanding is knowledge about the world that tells us that particular circumstances are situated in a larger flow of events, and that these events are somehow ordered. Life experience suggests that what actually happens usually has (some) meaning, that life is not a sequence of utterly random social interactions independent of one another, the way lottery numbers sequentially drawn make a winning series. Between what happened moments before and a few moments after there is *some* connection. And so, in addition to acquiring a specific image from which we can start a historical investigation, we infer that only *certain* things could have happened in the period under consideration, while other things, most likely, could not.

When confronted with an isolated image or a single fact we can always ask the question, So what? It offers nothing more than a departure point, which might eventually lead to general knowledge. But we should recognize that isolated facts and general knowledge also have a more direct relationship with one another. A fraction of a second, one photograph, possesses the power to invalidate an established narrative, in the way that a single experiment, a single counter-example in the natural sciences, compels us to reject an established theory.

When writing about the Holocaust we must be especially sensitive to the complexity of relationships between general knowledge and concrete events, because, more than other students of modern times, we must rely on personal documents. We have to draw on information pertaining to individual lives contained in diaries, letters, memoirs, photographs, and depositions made in courts or institutions established to document what happened to Jews during wartime. This is because those tasked with implementation of the Final Solution obfuscated their activities, destroying material evidence and trying to disguise and hide what they were doing. As a result, records of significant aspects of Nazi policies and their consequences do not exist. As Heinrich Himmler said to the top SS personnel of the Einsatzgruppen, who carried out mass executions of Jews behind the Eastern Front, congratulating them on work well done in a speech at Posen in October 1943, "The extermination of the Jewish people [is] a glorious page in our history that has never been written and is never to be written."[20] And so we must now find answers to questions such as how to convert episodic knowledge into a general understanding of what happened. How can information

---

[20] Ian Kershaw, *Hitler 1936–1945: Nemesis* (New York: Norton, 2000), 487.

about experiences of certain people be translated into a broader understanding of the epoch?

What we are investigating when focusing on the Holocaust are extremities of human behavior. The official documentation is scant and produced with an eye to misdirect and often to deceive. Hence trying to establish historical truth about this period requires a special effort. Given the kind of empirical material at our disposal, we cannot depict what happened to the Jews using the standard instruments of aggregating data, such as computing percentages (What proportion of Polish peasants were assisting Jews trying to hide in the countryside?); summing up individual cases to arrive at reliable global numerical estimates (How many Jews were killed by Polish peasants in the Podlasie region?); or computing the mean (What was the mean value of Jewish property taken over by a Polish neighbor in a given area?). In order to come to grips with what happened, we have to resort to more subtle methods of data presentation, including so-called thick description, commonly used in anthropology.[21]

In any case, both the type of sources available and the alien character of what Jews endured (that it was impossible to imagine or to convey to anyone who had not witnessed it directly is affirmed by virtually all chroniclers of the Shoah) suggest an analogy between Holocaust historians and anthropologists embarking on a study of remote tribes, relying on the expertise of local informants with whom they can communicate. Tales from the Holocaust arrive as if based on events that had taken place on some other continent altogether, reported by the faint and fragmented voices of a few survivors.

[21] Clifford Geertz, "Thick Description: Toward an Interpretive Theory of Culture," in *The Interpretation of Cultures: Selected Essays* (New York: Basic Books, 1973).

PHOTOGRAPHS AND DOCUMENTATION

THE GROUNDS OF EXTERMINATION
CAMPS IMMEDIATELY AFTER
THE WAR

To return to the photograph. The first mention of the Treblinka camp area after its liberation appears in a September 1944 report made by the Polish-Soviet Commission for Investigation of German Crimes. Shortly thereafter the Russian writer Vasili Grossman, who was working as a war correspondent, accompanied frontline troops of the Red Army and visited the camp with the Commission, then pieced together a very accurate description of how the death camp operated. Members of the Polish-Soviet Commission called in their report "for collecting and preserving all the documents to be found in the area and uncovering mass graves in order to reveal the secret of German crimes."[22]

But for many years thereafter no preservation efforts of any kind were pursued at Treblinka, other than the erection of a fence around the camp's perimeter in 1947. Appeals made in subsequent years for the protection and safeguarding of the area also went unheeded. Commemoration of the victims at the death camps—in Treblinka, Bełżec, and Sobibór—finally took place only in the 1960s. Trials of death-camp guards, which began at that time in Germany, may have been a factor, as Polish authorities worried that a court-ordered visit to the camps might reveal their condition of utter neglect.[23]

---

[22] Martyna Rusiniak, "Treblinka—Eldorado Podlasia?," *Kwartalnik Historii Żydów*, no. 2 (2006): 206.

[23] We should add that on no commemorating inscription in Chełmno, Sobibór, or Bełżec is it written that it was Jews who were the victims murdered in

One of the earliest statements about the postwar activities on the site of Treblinka was made by Michał Kalembasiak and Karol Ogrodowczyk, who visited the camp on September 12, 1945, and wrote a report. The entire area was scarred with recently dug pits, several of them meters deep, and human bones were scattered all around. People discovered sifting through the ashes didn't bother to answer when asked what they were doing. The scale of the excavations was so immense that Kalembasiak and Ogrodowczyk concluded that thousands of people had to have worked to produce this lunar landscape. "We want to add," they stated in a signed deposition for the Jewish Historical Commission in Warsaw, "that mutual relationships in the Treblinka area are simply incredible. People who enrich themselves with gold dug up from the graves by night plunder their own neighbors. We were terrified because in a peasant hut some dozen meters from the house where we spent the night, a woman was tortured with live fire to reveal the place where she was hiding gold and valuables."[24]

The writer Rachela Auerbach visited Treblinka on November 7, 1945, as part of an official delegation organized by the Main Commission for the Investigation of Hitlerite Crimes. She called one of the chapters of a small book she subsequently wrote about the Treblinka extermination camp "The Polish Colorado [she may have meant 'Eldorado'], or About the Gold Rush in Treblinka." She described how plunderers with shovels were everywhere. "They dig,

---

these camps. See Robert Kuwałek (former director of the museum in Bełżec), "Concentration and Death Camps as Places of Commemoration," a paper presented at the conference The Aftermath of the Holocaust, Poland 1944–2010, Yad Vashem, Jerusalem, October 3–6, 2010.

[24] Yad Vashem Archive, Jerusalem, 033/730.

they search, pulling out bones and body parts. Maybe something could still be found," she wrote, "maybe a golden tooth?"[25] The historian Józef Kermisz went to Treblinka several times in this period; in addition to crowds of local people "who were digging all over the sandy terrain," he also mentions "Soviet marauders," who detonated explosives in the camp area, "bombs from the [nearby military] airfield at Ceranów, [making] huge pits . . . that were filled with skulls, bones, and body parts which had not yet decomposed."[26]

Dominik Kucharek, a gleaner from Treblinka who had been served with an indictment for violating foreign-exchange laws—he tried to sell in Warsaw a diamond he found at Treblinka and purchase gold coins on the black market—explained in his deposition that "everybody" from his village went to dig there. "I didn't know that looking for gold and valuables at the site of the former camp at Treblinka was forbidden, because Soviet soldiers also went there with us to search. And they detonated explosives in places where they expected to find something."[27] There could be several hundred diggers working the camp at any one time. Given the size of the

---

[25] Rachela Auerbach's report on her visit to Treblinka was first published in *Dos Naje Leben*, no. 52, and later came out as a separate brochure, *Afn die felder fun Treblinka* (Centralna Żydowska Komisja Historyczna, Warsaw, 1947). The quote is from page 101. We are grateful to Natalia Aleksiun for translating it from the Yiddish.

[26] Dr. Józef Kermisz, *W Treblince po raz drugi*, Jewish Historical Institute (Żydowska Instytut Historyczny, ŻIH), Central Jewish Historical Commission (Centralna Zydowska Komisja Historyczna, CŻKH), 280/XX/pp. 56–72.

[27] According to the historian Martyna Rusiniak, this was the only indictment issued to a digger from Treblinka. In any case, Kucharek's indictment was quashed. Archiwum Powiatowe w Siedlcach, Akta w sprawie Dominika Kucharka, Sąd Okręgowy w Siedlcach, Wydział Karny (State Archives in Siedlce, Circuit Court in Siedlce, Criminal Division), sygn. 580.

site, approximating that of a sports stadium, it must have looked like a busy anthill. These digs went on for decades. "First clean-up and inventory activities at the site of the former camp began in the Spring of 1958," wrote a contemporary historian of Treblinka, Martyna Rusiniak. "During the initial cleaning it wasn't uncommon for the workers and the police to join occasionally with the diggers."[28] Testimonies from Bełżec tell a similar story. The main difference is that digging there had already begun during the war. Like Treblinka, Bełżec was dismantled by the Germans, the camp's terrain was plowed over, and trees and grass were planted to cover mass graves. Bełżec was the first death camp to close, in mid-1943. When the Germans got wind of what the Polish locals were doing, they chased them away and installed a permanent guard to make sure that no evidence of their own murderous activity would be unearthed.[29] As soon as the guard fled before the approaching Red Army, the local people resumed their excavations.

"According to information provided by policemen stationed in Bełżec," states a report prepared by a commission visiting Bełżec on October 10, 1945, "the area of the camp has been dug up by

---

[28] Martyna Rusiniak-Karwat, "Sąsiedzi byłego ośrodka masowej zagłady Treblinka II" (Neighbors of the former extermination camp Treblinka II), paper delivered at the Jewish Historical Institute in Warsaw, in manuscript.

[29] Records of investigation (Protokół przesłuchania) of Eugeniusz Goch, bricklayer from Bełżec, October 14, 1945, and of Maria Daniel from Bełżec, October 16, 1945, "Akta śledztwa w sprawie zbrodni popełnionych w obozie zagłady w Bełżcu" (Records of investigation concerning crimes perpetrated in the extermination camp at Bełżec), Archiwum Panstwowego Muzeum na Majdanku (Archives of the State Museum at Majdanek, APMM), sygn. XIX-1284.

local people looking for gold and precious stones left by murdered Jews. All over the dug-up terrain one finds scattered human bones: skulls, vertebrae, ribs, femurs, jaws, women's hair, often in braids, also fragments of rotting human flesh, such as hands or lower limbs of small children." The report notes that everywhere were scattered bones and ashes. "From deep pits wafts the smell of rotten human flesh. It all shows that the area of the camp along its northern and eastern perimeter is one big grave of people who had been murdered there." After the Germans fled from Bełżec the local police tried to inhibit digging in the camp area, "but it is difficult to do anything," explained the town's police precinct commander, Mieczysław Niedużak, "because as soon as one group of people is chased away, another group appears."[30]

The commission worked conscientiously, and in addition to talking to scores of witnesses the authors of the report also surveyed the camp. Nine separate sites in the death camp were probed for depth; in one instance the bottom of the grave was over twenty feet down. "When digging the probes it was ascertained that camp graves have been previously dug-up," and also "that at the present time the entire camp area is being dug up by the local population looking for valuables."[31]

[30] Commission report, October 10, 1945, and report of investigation of Mieczysław Niedużak, October 17, 1945, "Akta śledztwa w sprawie zbrodni popełnionych w obozie zagłady w Bełżcu," APMM, sygn. XIX-1284.

[31] "Protokół rozkopania cmentarzyska obozu śmierci w Bełżcu, October 12, 1945" and "Sprawozdanie z wyników dochodzenia w sprawie Obozu śmierci w Bełżcu" (Report on the results of investigation concerning the death-camp in Bełżec) in "Akta śledztwa w sprawie zbrodni popełnionych w obozie zagłady w Bełżcu," APMM, sygn. XIX–1284.

Death-camp harvesters usually worked alone, lest a lucky find provoke envy from a neighbor (remember the "incredible relationships" in the vicinity of Treblinka, where diggers were robbed and tortured one another). Both in Bełżec and in Treblinka it was common practice to take skulls home in order to check them out later, and "in peace."[32]

There were also a few entrepreneurs who hired small crews to dig for them, such as a man known as the "banker of Bełżec," who owned a brick factory in town and staked a claim to an area where a latrine had been previously situated in the camp. It was the most fertile spot, presumably because desperate Jews who figured out at last what awaited them threw valuables therein instead of surrendering them to camp officials.[33] After the Red Army liberated the area near Sobibór, Soviet soldiers scooped out the former camp

[32] Ewa Czerwiakowska, "Głos z otchłani" (Voice from the depth), *Karta*, no. 59/2009 p. 103. See the documentary film, *Bełżec*, by Guillaume Moscovitz for similar practices in Bełżec and personal information from Agnieszka Grudzińska, who translated interviews with Bełżec inhabitants for the film.

[33] One of the few artifacts uncovered at the Bełżec site was an inscription on a wooden board directing people to hold on to their documents and valuables after they had undressed, and to give them in deposit to an official at "a window." *Bełżec: The Nazi Camp for Jews in the Light of Archeological Sources* (Washington, D.C.: Council for the Protection of Memory of Combat and Martyrdom and the United States Holocaust Memorial Museum, 2000), figure 9, p. 12. Other artifacts found at Bełżec were "304 pieces of concrete rings with the diameter of about 6 cm and 1 cm thickness on which 5 number figures had been pressed. In upper parts of these rings small holes were stated [?], which probably served to hang them" (p. 57; see also figures 115 and 117, pp. 83, 84). It is unclear what they were used for, but they might have been given—as part of continuing camouflage of the real purpose of the camp—in exchange for the deposit to be retrieved later. Such relatively large concrete rings could be easily swept from the floor of a gas chamber, cleaned, and used again.

latrine with buckets, hauling out loads of wristwatches.[34] The latrine area in Bełżec also yielded small skeletons, most likely of Jewish children who had been drowned there by camp guards.

The journal of a nationalist guerrilla unit active in Podlasie one year after the end of the war mentions collecting "contributions" from people who were digging through Jewish ashes at Treblinka.[35] Thus "Jewish gold" that had been missed by the Third Reich ended up, through informal taxation imposed on gleaners, also financing the anticommunist underground in Poland.[36]

THE BONES

Although the photograph remains mysterious and troubling, it can be classified as a "euphemism": the horror behind it appears as something peaceful. The observer's eye stops first on the group

[34] Yahad in Unum Archive, Paris, deposition 31P, part 1.

[35] *NSZ na Podlasiu w walce z systemem komunistycznym w latach 1944–1952* (Struggle against the communist system in the years 1944–1952 by NSZ, Nationalist Armed Forces, in Podlasie), ed. Mariusz Bechta and Leszek Żebrowski (Siedlce: Związek Żołnierzy NSZ, 1998), 201.

[36] In the chronicle of a Home Army unit from Wilno, which moved into the vicinity of Treblinka in February 1946, we read that when partisans were apprised of the practice of digging through the necropolis of Treblinka by local peasants, the unit sent patrols over on three nights, on February 4, 5, and 6, 1946, to Wólka Okrąglik to apprehend the diggers and punish them with a solid lashing (*ukarano solidnymi batami*). See podziemiezbrojne.blox.pl/2011/01/6-Brygada-Wileńska-AK-a-Złote-żniwa.html.

of people, and only then moves down; we need a moment to understand what is lying on the ground in front of the group. We have here an encounter of two orders of things. On one level, there are living, vibrant individuals, life and movement; on the other, immobile skulls and bones—almost objects, things. In many cultures, the encounter of these two orders—the living and the dead—is ritualized; it happens in clearly defined situations, to which the scene depicted on our photograph does not belong. The dead body is usually hidden in a coffin or covered by a shroud. It is promptly buried or burned; otherwise its smell invades daily life. Bones, if visible at all, are used for science or teaching, as part of a skeleton, maintaining in this way a definable shape; or they are made to form a skull and crossbones, which is meant to warn against danger, most often poison, piracy, or high-voltage electric wires.

In the Christian tradition, the skull and crossbones serve as memento mori, a symbol of Golgotha: the skull at the foot of the Cross represents our forefather Adam. All of this was certainly known to the people in the photo, as they are most certainly Catholic. It is striking that the skull and crossbones are placed in the very middle of a row of human bones, and that the people have formed a semicircle symmetrically around it. In a professional photograph, perhaps, the skull and crossbones would constitute its focal point; in this one, they are in the forefront. We look at the people; the bones are hidden in full sight.

This tidying up of the skulls and bones into a memento mori, so that they would automatically provide a warning or be inscribed into the religious (Christian) order of the world, seems an attempt to normalize this horrible scene, part of an effort to give it meaning. One needs to admire the probably spontaneous gesture by a person or persons, most likely women, who put the bones in a row, crossed them, and therefore "Christianized" these Jewish remains. This was the symbolic dictionary that the tidying ones had available while dealing with human bones.

THE DEATH CAMPS AND THE LOCAL POPULATION

The practice of digging for Jewish gold was described in postwar Polish literature.[37] Even so, it was not highlighted and therefore not absorbed by those who did not witness the Shoah. Not only was such an activity (as well as other war-time preoccupations, like massive denunciations)[38] too distant from everyday reality, but the writers were constrained by the accepted postwar narrative, according to which it was the non-Jewish citizens of Poland who were victimized. And it seems, even today, indecent to blame the victims.[39]

[37] See Jacek Leociak, "Poeta pamięta" (The poet remembers), Znak 3 (2011): 19–29.

[38] See Sławomir Buryła, "Proza współczesna o donosach i donosicielach" (Contemporary prose about denunciations and denouncers), in Zagłada: Współczesne problemy rozumienia i przedstawiania (Shoah: Contemporary problems of understanding and representation), ed. P. Czapliński and E. Domańska (Poznań: Studia Polonistyczne, 2009), 209–230.

[39] There were exceptions, of course. The most famous poem about Poles' denunciation of Jews and the resulting pillage of Jewish property (not translated into English) is "Non Omnis Moriar," by Zuzanna Ginczanka, who had been denounced herself and was killed during the war.

The war left a specialized vocabulary in Polish: *szmalcownik* (someone blackmailing Jews for money), *szaber* (appropriation of "post-Jewish" [*pożydowska*] or "post-German" [*poniemiecka*] property),[40] and *kenkarta* (a German-issued ID). But the practice of digging up the camps in search of valuables did not gain a proper name. "Diggers" does not express the horror of what they are actually doing: digging up and examining rotting human remains and ashes. A different term, "dentists," was used in Warsaw to describe people who looked for gold teeth in the skulls dug out of a Warsaw Jewish cemetery.[41] Sometimes *kanadziarz* ("Canada-man") is used—for

[40] This neologism appears in the Polish language only in three versions as "post-Jewish," "post-German," and, more rarely, "post-manor" property. Expressions such as "post-French" or "post-British" property, for example, would be considered simply linguistic mistakes. Due to historical circumstances, there were in Poland two cases of massive appropriation of other people's property in the twentieth century: following the expulsion of the German population after the war and after the extermination of the Jews. (The term "post-manor" denotes property confiscated by the state from land owners and nobility.) But because murder or expulsion does not transfer ownership to anything, and especially to the possessions accumulated by generations, "post-Jewish" is only a *façon de parler* and does not define ownership. This is well known to the inhabitants of small Polish towns, who responded with anxiety to the appearance of any stranger lest it was a Jew or, in certain areas, a German, who came to reclaim what rightfully belonged to him.

[41] In her memoir, Vladke Meed described how, right after the war, she went to the Jewish cemetery in Warsaw to visit the grave of her father. The cemetery was devastated, with "overturned tombstones, desecrated graves, and scattered near them skulls, human skulls. . . . Although you know that these are signs of the ghoulish handiwork of the so-called 'dentists'—Poles who were seeking gold teeth in the mouths of Jewish corpses—you feel somehow strangely guilty, deeply humiliated, ashamed that you, too belong to the species called the 'human race.'" Quoted in Gabriel N. Finder and Judith R. Cohen, "*Memento Mori*, Photographs from the Grave," *Polin: Studies in Polish Jewry* 20 (2008): 57.

example, in an interview with Marek Kucia, the author of a book about Auschwitz.[42] This term belongs to the curious language called *Lagersprache*, "camp-speak."[43]

The area surrounding the death camps was indeed, as Rachela Auerbach suggested, a Polish Colorado—on account of what happened not afterward but during the war. Villages in the vicinities of camps prospered materially as a result of trade between the camp guards and the local people, trade that brought a "material and economic revolution" to this area.[44] A landlord whose property was not far from Treblinka put it thus: "Thatched roofs were gone,

---

[42] In his interview in *Tygodnik Powszechny* (December 28, 2009), Marek Kucia said, "Even in the 1980s, on the terrain of the former camp, so-called *kanadziarze* were active, who, in search of gold, were digging over the grounds around the crematoria and around the places where the ashes of victims were thrown in." The interview was conducted after the theft of the sign hanging at the entrance of the camp. Professor Kucia said, as if explaining the reasons for the activities of *kanadziarze*, "They were searchers of treasures, who looked for valuables sold later on the market. But I never heard about a theft of a [Auschwitz] museum's showpiece." The term *Kanada*, as it appears in the concentration camp stories by Tadeusz Borowski, was applied to the job of unloading the new prisoners' transports coming into the camps and sorting their luggage. It is quite surprising that it would be used to designate postwar diggers. "Canada" is not a synonym for "Eldorado" anymore, and the biting irony of the original use of this word is lost on contemporary listeners. The prisoners working on Auschwitz Kanada were most often also destined for death. Their enjoyment of the goods of the dead was to last but a moment.

[43] D. Wesołowska, *Słowa z piekieł rodem: Lagersprache* (Words from Hell: Lagersprache) (Kraków: Oficyna Wydawnicza Impuls, 1996). Since the prisoners arrived prepared for resettlement, they usually brought food, valuables, money, everything that their foresight told them to take. While they were unloaded (this too is a euphemism; one should rather say while they were thrown out of the train cars, stripped of their goods and clothes, selected for death and killed) the prisoner engaged in these activities could fill his stomach, dress his body, gain some valuables.

[44] Jerzy Królikowski, *Wspomnienie z okolic Treblinki w czasie okupacji* (Reminiscences from the Treblinka's vicinity during the occupation), ŻIH, 302/224, p. 29.

replaced by sheet metal, and the entire village seemed like a piece of Europe suddenly moved into the center of Podlasie."[45] What lay behind this perceptive observation? In addition to a small staff of SS men, Treblinka's personnel was made up of released Soviet POWs, mostly Ukrainians, trained by the SS to serve as guards.[46] Those young men, about a hundred of them altogether, treated with contempt by their German superiors, were called by the locals *Wachman* or, alternatively, "Blacks," from the color of their uniforms. They easily communicated in pidgin Polish-Ukrainian with the local people and were welcome guests in their homes.[47] The reason was that they had money and valuables.

Treblinka guards traded with the locals, buying alcohol, tasty food, and sex, and the inflow of capital into the area was beyond anything that had happened there before or has happened since. In other places local inhabitants merely took property belonging to local Jews (often as impecunious as themselves). In Treblinka, Bełżec, and Sobibór over a million and a half Jews were murdered, including the Jewish population of several large cities. Money as well as valuables, which Jews took on their final journey, hoping

---

[45] Jan Górski, "Na przełomie dziejów" (At the threshold of a new epoch), ed. Jan Grabowski, *Zagłada Żydów*, no. 2 (2006): 286. A similar phenomenon in a village called Żłobek (Kindergarten) near the Sobibór camp is reported by a peasant interviewed by Father Debois (Yahad in Unum Archive, Paris, interview 31P, part 2).

[46] The training was done at a special camp at Trawniki, and those who received it are sometimes called in the literature Trawniki-men, or Trawnikis.

[47] Two local residents, both women, interviewed during the investigation concerning crimes committed at Bełżec, reported that camp guards regularly took meals at their houses. See also Królikowski, *Wspomnienie z okolic Treblinki w czasie okupacji*, 30. For example Mieczysław Chodźko, who was a prisoner at Treblinka, writes that SS men mistreated Ukrainian guards, punished them with lashes, and took away their weapons at night (ŻIH, 302/321).

against hope that they might survive, in some small part trickled into the hands of the locals. The Warsaw native and engineer Jerzy Królikowski, who lived in the village of Treblinka while supervising construction of a railroad bridge nearby, recalled that "wrist watches were sold by the dozens, for pennies, and local peasants carried them in egg baskets offering them to whomever was interested."[48]

Villages around extermination camps were swept up in a gold rush akin to that in the Wild West. "Prostitutes from a nearby town, or even from Warsaw, showed up, eager to get golden coins, while vodka and food could be purchased in numerous houses."[49] "In villages close to the camp, Ukrainians, during their spare time from 'work,' were heartily welcomed by some peasants. Daughters in such households, people were saying, provided company to these murderers and eagerly benefited from their largesse."[50] A peasant from Z łobek put on a big smile when reminiscing to Father Debois on camera, about beautiful singing by Ukrainian guards from the nearby Sobibór who used to visit local girls.[51]

The local population was determined not to be outdone by outsiders in the provision of desired services. Camp guards paid for food and vodka "without counting the change," and only by the time Treblinka was about to close did they start "selling diamonds by carats and not by piece."[52] A local informant whom we have already quoted (a well-educated prewar supporter of the National Democratic Party and a landowner from Ceranów)

[48] Królikowski, *Wspomnienie z okolic Treblinki*, 30.
[49] Mieczysław Chodźko, ŻIH, 302/321, p. 47.
[50] Królikowski, *Wspomnienie z okolic Treblinki w czasie okupacji*, 30.
[51] Yahad ad Unum Archive, Paris, deposition 31P, part 2.
[52] Królikowski, *Wspomnienie z okolic Treblinki w czasie okupacji*, 30.

described the circumstances in even more derisive terms: "The village Wólka Okrąglik is situated near Treblinka. Peasants from there used to send their wives and daughters to meet with Ukrainian guards employed at the camp. They were beside themselves if the women did not bring, in exchange for personal services, enough jewelry and valuables that belonged to the Jews. Theirs was a very profitable business."[53] On occasion more permanent relationships evolved. One of the guards in Bełżec married a local girl, for example.

Mieczysław Chodźko, a Treblinka survivor, reveals in his reminiscences another interesting detail. "Guards," he writes, "had cameras and took pornographic pictures, which they very much liked to show to each other."[54] This may help explain some of the mystery of the photograph. Just as it is unknown who took the picture or why, it was initially puzzling that a camera made it into Podlasie countryside shortly after the war in the first place. Now we know that both during and after the war it was possible to find virtually anything in the vicinity of Treblinka. The area flourished during the camp's existence. "Local dives for Ukrainians were getting more and more prosperous in neighbouring villages," recalled Jerzy Królikowski. "Some enterprising folks were bringing specialty food and exclusive pre-war liquors from Warsaw and, in the spring of 1943, early-season delicacies appeared on the market"[55]

The inhabitants of Treblinka and its surroundings did not draw their income exclusively from the dead Jews. Their business

---

[53] Górski, "Na przełomie dziejów," 286–287.
[54] Mieczysław Chodźko, ŻIH, 302/321, p. 47.
[55] Królikowski, *Wspomnienie z okolic Treblinki w czasie okupacji*, 31.

activities started the moment trains filled with living Jews destined for gas chambers stopped at the Treblinka train station. Huge trains sixty cars long arriving from Warsaw were filled with the condemned, who could not be disposed of at once because of the limited capacity of the gas chambers. These trains had to be split into smaller sections and rolled into the camp sequentially. Even when everything went smoothly, freight cars filled with victims awaiting their turn to be killed were parked in the station for hours. It also happened that two or three trains might reach Treblinka at the same time. And whenever a train arrived at dusk it would be kept in the station till the next morning.[56]

After a train arrived, writes Królikowski, people from neighboring villages would come to the station.

When I saw people near the train for the first time I thought that they came out with a noble intent to feed the hungry and bring water to the thirsty. But I was quickly told by the workers [on the construction project, which Królikowski supervised] with whom I spoke that this was regular commercial activity, selling water and food at very profitable prices. And indeed this is what it was, as I later found out. When transports were not guarded by German gendarmerie, which didn't allow anybody to approach the trains, but by one of the auxiliary police formations [occasionally even by the Polish police] crowds would assemble, bringing pails of water and bottles of moonshine. Water was for the people locked up

---

[56] Ząbecki, *Wspomnienia dawne i nowe*, 47. Ząbecki was a train dispatcher at the Treblinka station, and his memoirs dovetail with many details in the reminiscences of the engineer Królikowski.

in freight cars, while liquor was used to bribe the convoy guards, so they would allow the locals to approach the train. When there was no liquor, or convoy guards would not be satisfied with this form of payment, girls would come forward, put arms around their necks and cover them with kisses—anything in order to be able to come close to the wagons.

After permission was granted, trade with unfortunate prisoners dying of thirst and willing to pay 100 zlotys for a cup of water began. Apparently, it happened occasionally that people took the money but did not hand over the water. In the meantime, convoy guards would drink hooch and then engage in their "games" with trapped and suffering prisoners, which I described before.[57]

The "games" consisted of the drunken convoy guards accepting bribes from the Jews to let them escape, and then shooting at them when they tried to run away. "Sometimes train escorts overdid it and got so drunk that they couldn't aim their guns and some people actually managed to escape."[58] A railroad employee, a train dispatcher from Treblinka, adds in his memoirs that "when convoy

[57] Królikowski, *Wspomnienie z okolic Treblinki w czasie okupacji*, 31, 32.
[58] Królikowski, *Wspomnienie z okolic Treblinki w czasie okupacji*, 32. "At the end of September we got so endangered by increasingly frequent shoot outs that we had to take preventive measures. In the first place I sent my wife, who was sharing my life in this frightening area, back to Warsaw. She was much more endangered than myself because she was at home for the entire day, and they shot in this direction from the station. . . . All the employees who took residence in Treblinka (and they were numerous, since this was the closest village to the construction site) stopped using the road on the way to work, because it ran along the railroad tracks and the station. We went through small paths, and across meadows, taking a much longer way but at least we no longer had to take cover and fall on the ground when shots were fired" (15).

guards spent all their bullets they would run after the people trying to escape and kill them with rifle butts, bayonets, and even iron rods or pitchforks that they grabbed from nearby peasant farms."[59] Drunk escort troops played their games especially with Jews on trains detained in the station overnight, and as a result a number of Jews died before they ever reached the gas chambers. "During the day corpses were collected in the station, piled on several platform-wagons and taken into the death camp,"[60] to be thrown into mass graves or burned. After the ghetto uprising in Warsaw in May 1943, writes Królikowski, "gunfire during train arrivals got so heavy, as if a military operation was in progress."[61]

About a hundred trains reached Treblinka from Warsaw alone. Altogether many hundreds passed through the station on their way to the camp. And income from the "trading" with the Jews, alongside profits from selling food, alcohol, and sex to camp guards, revolutionized the local economy.[62] A resident of

[59] Ząbecki, *Wspomnienia dawne i nowe*, 48.

[60] Ząbecki, *Wspomnienia dawne i nowe*, 47.

[61] Królikowski, *Wspomnienie z okolic Treblinki w czasie okupacji*, 15.

[62] The same sort of commercial activity was pursued by railroad men whenever opportunity arose. The engineer Henryk Bryskier, who was a captain in the Polish army and a former member of Józef Piłsudski's Legions (from the time of World War I), was deported during the uprising. "Near Targówek," he writes, "the train stopped and trucks from the Tobbens Company brought some bread. It was the first meal we got in 48 hours. While the train was there Polish railroad men, permitted to do so by the escort troops, brought kettles of water and kept handing bottles full of water to hands which eagerly were reaching through wagon windows taking for half a liter, 100 zlotys. Before the train was back in motion, each 'merciful' railroad man collected a few thousand zlotys. . . . I was standing by the window and I was passing back and forth water and money" (ŻIH, 302/90). Jerzy Pfeffer describes an identical transaction when a transport of Jews to the Majdanek camp stopped at the train station in Lublin (ŻIH, 302/23).

Bełżec opined after the war that it had been very difficult for people in her area to "keep their decency" during the German occupation.[63]

Such profiteering by people living near the sites of mass murder was not specific to Poland. Kazimierz Sakowicz lived at the edge of the Ponary forest, near Vilnius, today's capital of Lithuania, where 100,000 people were shot during the war, roughly 80 percent of them Jews. Three days after Lithuanians began to execute Jews in Ponary, Sakowicz noted in his diary, "Since July 14 [the victims] have been stripped to their underwear. Brisk business in clothing." Then, on August 1–2, "For the Germans 300 Jews are 300 enemies of humanity; for the Lithuanians they are 300 pairs of shoes, trousers, and the like." "Since August 22," he wrote in another entry, "the Germans have been taking the valuables, leaving the Lithuanians with the clothes and the like."[64]

Sakowicz writes sparingly, noting facts in a tightly controlled and restrained manner. But occasionally he also sketched a more elaborate scene:

> November 21. . . . A Shaulist [Lithuanian volunteer working with the Nazis] with a rifle left the base and on the road (it was market day—Friday) he began to sell women's clothing: a few topcoats, dresses and galoshes. He sold the last pair of coats, navy blue and brown, for 120 rubles and as a "bonus" he also threw in a pair of galoshes. When one of the peasants

---

[63] Communication from Robert Kuwałek, former director of the museum in Bełżec.

[64] Kazimierz Sakowicz, *Ponary Diary, 1941–1943: A Bystander's Account of Mass Murder* (New Haven, Conn.: Yale University Press, 2005), 13, 16, 19.

(Wacław Tankun of Stary Międzyrzecz) asked whether he would still sell [him something for his wife], the Shaulist replied. "Let them wait" and he would "choose" a Jewish woman exactly her size.

Tankun and his wife were horrified, and when the Shaulist left they went away quickly. The Shaulist reappeared with the clothing. He was angry that the "yokels" weren't there because he had "gone to the trouble" of choosing a Jewish woman from the fourth line whose height was about that of the villager's.[65]

Things will go on like this for several years:

Thursday, October 7 [1943]

Since morning, near the crossing, a market for the effects of yesterday's victims. . . .

October 11

The constant shootings, practically every day, have caused the Lithuanians who trade effects to be at the crossing permanently, day and night. They drink entire nights away.

Wednesday, October 13

The Shaulists are waiting for something, because there will be a group. . . . And the merchants also wait. They are not disappointed. At about 12 in the afternoon a truck.[66]

[65] Sakowicz, *Ponary Diary*, 40.
[66] Sakowicz, *Ponary Diary*, 129, 131, 133.

TENDING ONE'S GARDEN

"Since Homer," Theodor Adorno writes, "the concepts of good and wealth are intertwined in the Greek language. Christianity first negated that identification, in the phrase that it would be easier to pass a camel through the eye of a needle than for a rich person to enter heaven. But the particular theological premise on voluntary chosen poverty indicates how deeply the general consciousness is stamped by the ethos of property. . . . To be good and to have goods coincided from the beginning."[67] Things, even those of little value, are good in themselves, because they are a result of work, of effort. And they are useful. At home, in the garden, everything can be utilized.

People have long despoiled the bodies of the victims of catastrophe or of dead soldiers on battlefields, a practice with a family resemblance to what is going on in our photo. It was a common phenomenon, for example, during the Napoleonic wars; Stendhal described it powerfully in the fourth chapter of *The Charterhouse of Parma*. It was also common during World War II and perhaps during most of the wars in history. In her book about the American Civil War, the historian Drew Gilpin Faust includes an illustration from a contemporary paper showing the "Rebel Soldiers after Battle 'Peeling' (i.e. Stripping) the Fallen Union Soldiers." "Soldiers desperate for clothing robbed the dead with little feeling of

---

[67] Theodor Adorno, "Model Virtue," in *Minima Moralia: Reflections from the Damaged Life*, trans. Dennis Redmond (2005), chapter 119, http://download1098. mediafire.com (accessed November 21, 2011).

propriety or remorse," she writes, "and thieves and scavengers appeared on battlefields immediately after the end of hostilities. At the end of the Battle of Franklin in 1864, needy Confederate soldiers even stripped the bodies of their own generals, six of whom lay dead on the field." The nearby population stripped everything that seemed useful.[68] Stressing the neediness of the soldiers, Faust seems to be saying that the dead do not use things. Yet she does call those who disrobed cadavers "hyenas," thus reducing them to the level of animals.

It can be safely assumed that the customs of every social and ethnic group demand respect toward their dead. Such respect is not a sign of some "higher" civilization, but of basic human solidarity. The body is not a thing; even after death it retains the shape of the person whom it was serving in life. What's more, many religions, including Catholicism, believe in bodily resurrection and therefore attach great importance to burial. Thus one cannot say that the despoiling of "the bottomless Treblinka earth," as Vasili Grossman described it,[69] could be justified by poverty, need, or necessity.

A better assessment can be found in Zygmunt Bauman's idea that the Shoah was a result of a "gardener's" vision of society, a vision in which some people are considered weeds and efforts to

---

[68] Drew Gilpin Faust, *This Republic of Suffering: Death and the American Civil War* (New York: Knopf, 2008), 74–75.

[69] This is how Treblinka was described by Vasili Grossman. When, walking on the territory of the camp, Grossman stumbled upon clusters of human hair, he wrote, "Then it is all true! . . . And it seems the heart must surely burst under the weight of sorrow, grief and pain that is beyond human endurance." Vassily Grossman, *The Treblinka Hell*, ed. Gershon Aharoni (Tel Aviv, 1984), 29. But in the words of Czesław Miłosz, "The heart doesn't die when one thinks it should" ("Elegy for N.N.").

eliminate them rational, purposeful. The persistent, decades-long digging, raking, sifting through the camp areas can be seen as constituting such "gardening" activities. These activities—digging out human bodies, ashes, and bones in search of valuables—are performed outside of any moral context. These places are not considered burial grounds but fields open to gleaners.

THE TAKING OF JEWISH PROPERTY BY ORDINARY PEOPLE

In current legal disputes concerning the ownership of art objects that belonged to Jews before the Nazis came to power, "forced sales" (defined as transactions that would not have taken place had there been no Nazi rule) are being litigated. Lawyers for Jewish art owners and their heirs continue to argue that along with Aryanization forced sale was a method of plunder disguised as a legitimate transaction.

The principle would apply to more than the sale of art objects, or, for that matter, businesses and luxurious villas. Poor Jews selling their furniture, bedding, assorted household goods, or winter clothes to Aryan neighbors for pennies had also been plundered. If anything, their losses were more dramatic because they brought on life-threatening pauperization. Simply put, those who availed themselves of the opportunities to acquire Jewish property for less than its real worth because there was Nazi rule, no matter how (un)valuable it was to begin with, partook in the spoliation of European Jewry. This applies not just to governments, museums, galleries, and entrepreneurs, but to millions of ordinary people who fleeced their neighbors.[70]

But, as we know, the population of occupied Europe did not take over Jewish property solely by legal means, whether through forced sales or Aryanization decrees. In Radziłów, as an eyewitness told a journalist sixty years later, it was more difficult to name townspeople who did *not* plunder Jewish houses while their inhabitants were being incinerated in a large barn on the outskirts of town on July 7, 1941. Everybody seemed to be in the streets grabbing what they could. In the well-known diary of Dr. Zygmunt Klukowski from Szczebrzeszyn—and hence from another part of the country—we read, "A lot of [peasants in] wagons came from the countryside and stood waiting the entire day for the moment when they could start looting [as rumors had it that Jews would be

---

[70] In the first volume of *Nazi Germany and the Jews*, Saul Friedlander describes a scene from Witlich, a small town in the Moselle Valley, on the morning following the Kristallnacht: "Jewish businesses were vandalized, Jewish men beaten up and taken away. Herr Marx, who owned the butcher shop down the street, was one of the half dozen Jewish men already on the truck. The SA men were laughing at Frau Marx who stood in front of her smashed plate-glass window [with] both hands raised in bewildered despair. 'Why are you people doing this to us?' she wailed at the circle of silent faces in the windows, her lifelong neighbors. 'What have we ever done to you?'" Saul Friedlander, *Nazi Germany and the Jews* (New York: Harper Perennial, 1998), 1:278.

Decades later, after Friedlander gave a public lecture in Hamburg, a young man came up to him passing on greetings from his grandmother from Witlich. To Friedlander's uncomprehending stare, he answered that his grandmother was a neighbor of Frau Marx. When looted Jewish belongings were sold at bargain prices to local residents, she acquired a pillow from Frau Marx's household, and it now weighed heavily on her conscience. She kept the pillow buried deep in a closet at home and would very much have liked Friedlander to tell her how she should dispose of it. Friedlander recounted the story during his public lectures at the Remarque Institute in New York City on October 12 and 13, 1999.

'resettled' on that day]. News keeps reaching us from all directions about the scandalous behavior of segments of the local population who rob emptied Jewish apartments. I am sure our little town will be no different."[71] Indeed in October, after another *Aktion*, Klukowski returns to the subject of plunder when he records in his diary, "The population grabs from opened Jewish houses anything they can get hold of. People shamelessly carry big bundles with pitiful Jewish belongings or merchandise from small Jewish shops."[72] In Jedwabne on July 10, 1941, "the barn was still burning, when some inhabitants hurried to plunder Jewish belongings."[73]

Things were not much different at the other end of Europe. When the oldest Greek Jewish community was deported from Salonica, "as soon as they were marched away, people rushed into their houses, tore up floorboards and battered down walls and ceilings, hoping to find hidden valuables. There was a 'complete breakdown of

---

[71] Zygmunt Klukowski, *Dziennik z lat okupacji zamojszczyzny* (Journal from the years of occupation of the Zamość region) (Lublin: Ludowa Spółdzielnia Wydawnicza, 1958), entry of April 13, 1942.

[72] Klukowski, *Dziennik z lat okupacji zamojszczyzny*, 255, 292.

[73] Stanislaw Przechodzki, "Szatan wstąpił do Jedwabnego" (Devil came to Jedwabne), *Gazeta Wyborcza*, April 5, 2001. On July 10, 1941, a mass murder of the Jewish population in the town of Jedwabne, situated in the eastern part of Poland, was carried out by their Catholic neighbors. Some 1,600 people were killed on that day, which culminated in chasing all the Jews that were still alive into a barn, which was then set on fire. There is an extensive literature on the subject; see especially Jan T. Gross, *Neighbors: The Destruction of the Jewish Community in Jedwabne, Poland* (Princeton, N.J.: Princeton University Press, 2001); Antony Polonsky and Joanna B. Michlic, eds., *The Neighbors Respond: The Controversy over the Jedwabne Massacre in Poland* (Princeton, N.J.: Princeton University Press, 2004). See also Paweł Machcewicz and Krzysztof Persak, eds., *Wokół Jedwabnego*, 2 vols. (Warsaw: Instytut Pamięci Narodowej, 2002); Anna Bikont, *My z Jedwabnego* (We from Jedwabne) (Warsaw: Prószyński i S-ka, 2004).

order' wrote an official at the time, and the second-hand shops of the city began to fill up with stolen goods."[74]

It is impossible to state how many people benefited materially from ethnic cleansing carried out during the German occupation. A Polish historian estimated at half a million "those who got ownership titles in Jewish *shtetls*."[75] He had in mind land, houses, stores, and farms taken over by the local people rather than what Klukowski called "pitiful Jewish belongings." But furniture, farm equipment, household goods, toys, eiderdowns, cushions, and clothes (which were often referred to as "Jewish rags") did not disappear from the face of the earth, and only some of these items were shipped as booty to Germany.

The takeover of Jewish property was so widespread in occupied Poland that it called for the emergence of rules determining distribution. Thus when in August 1941 a certain Helena Klimaszewska went from the hamlet of Goniądz to Radziłów "to get an apartment for her husband's parents because she knew that after the liquidation of the Jews there are empty apartments,"[76] she was told on arrival that a certain "Godlewski decides what to do with 'post-Jewish' apartments." She presented her request to him but, as she later testified in court, "Godlewski replied, 'don't even think

[74] Mark Mazower, *Salonica: City of Ghosts. Christians, Muslims and Jews 1430–1950* (London: HarperCollins, 2004), 443, 444.

[75] Wojciech Lizak, "Z perspektywy ludu" (From ordinary people's perspective), *Tygodnik Powszechny*, no. 45 (2004).

[76] Radziłów is situated some ten kilometers from Jedwabne, and on July 7, 1941 (three days before the Jedwabne murder), several hundred local Jews were murdered there by the local population. Indeed Jedwabne may be considered a copycat crime following the Radziłów example, where the local residents also burned their Jewish neighbors in a barn.

about it.' When I said that Mr. Godlewski has four houses at his disposal and I don't have even one he replied 'this is none of your business, I am awaiting a brother returning from Russia where the Soviets deported him and he has to have a house.' When I insisted that I need an apartment, he replied 'when people were needed to kill the Jews you weren't here, and now you want an apartment,'" an argument that met with a strong rebuttal from Klimaszewska's mother-in-law: "They don't want to give an apartment, but they sent my grandson to douse the barn with gasoline" (referring to the barn in Radziłów).[77] And so, we are witnessing a conversation between an older woman and other adults that is premised on the assumption that one gains a right to valuable goods by taking part in the murder of their owners.

ABOUT THE KILLING OF JEWS

Poland was divided by Stalin and Hitler in September 1939, and for the next twenty months a temporary border between the USSR and the Third Reich ran more or less along the rivers San

---

[77] Her grandson, Józef Ekstowicz, together with another youth climbed on the roof of the barn in Radziłów where several hundred Jews had been pushed in by their neighbors. Then they doused it with gasoline and the building was set on fire. Andrzej Żbikowski, "Pogromy i mordy ludności żydowskiej w Łomżyńskiem i na Białostocczyźnie latem 1941 roku w świetle relacji ocalałych Żydów i dokumentów sądowych" (Pogroms and killings of the Jewish population in Łomża and Białystok area in light of Jewish recollections and court documents), in Machcewicz and Persak, *Wokół Jedwabnego*, 1:244.

and Bug, cutting the prewar Polish state down the middle.[78] And since the Nazis began the mass killings of the Jews following Hitler's attack against the Soviet Union in June 1941, the first wave of murders on the Eastern Front took place in the prewar territory of Poland. It was in those circumstances that on July 10, 1941, the inhabitants of Jedwabne murdered their Jewish neighbors. Similar crimes occurred that summer and early autumn in about two dozen villages and small towns of the Bialystok voievodeship.[79] It turns out that in response to encouragement by the Nazi Einsatzgruppen, local people joined in murderous assaults on their Jewish fellow citizens. Reports filed by the Polish

[78] On August 23, 1939, Nazi Germany and the Soviet Union concluded a treaty of nonaggression, known in historiography as the Ribbentrop-Molotov Pact, after the names of the foreign ministers who signed the document in Moscow. A week later, on September 1, 1939, World War II began. As agreed between the signatories, the Red Army marched into Poland soon after the German attack (it did so on September 17). In the secret protocols attached to the August treaty, the Soviet Union reserved for itself a "sphere of interests" including Bessarabia, Estonia, Latvia, and the better part of Poland. The original demarcation line between the Nazi and the Soviet zones of occupation—splitting the capital city, Warsaw, in half along the Vistula River—appeared in the September 25, 1939, issue of the main Soviet newspaper, *Pravda*.

On September 28 in Moscow the German-Soviet Boundary and Friendship Treaty was signed, and a somewhat modified territorial division of recent conquests was agreed upon. Stalin settled for only half of Poland's territory and drew the frontier eastward (it ran, in part, along the rivers Bug and San). In exchange for giving up a good chunk of Poland, including half of the capital city, he consolidated his grip on the Baltic states by bringing Lithuania, Latvia, and Estonia into the Soviet fold.

[79] Paweł Machcewicz, "Wokół Jedwabnego," in Machcewicz and Persak, *Wokół Jedwabnego*, 1:31–35.

anti-Nazi underground organizations documented such events as they were taking place.[80]

Armed volunteers and vigilante groups that emerged during the period of transition from Soviet to Nazi occupation later joined elements of administration and auxiliary police created by the Germans. And until the Nazi rule came to an end, Ukrainians, Lithuanians, Latvians, Estonians, Russians, Belorussians, and Poles staffed various security details—called different things in different parts of the occupied territories—that were involved in tracking down and killing Jews.

In addition to an unspecified number of so-called *Schutzmanner*, people of Polish extraction who volunteered for the German gendarmerie, the main auxiliary force in the territory of the Generalgouvernement, or GG, was the so-called dark-blue or Polish police (*granatowa policja*). Made up in the vast majority by prewar Polish state policemen, it was responsible, in the opinion of Emmanuel Ringelblum, for murdering "tens of thousands" of

[80] Here are two quotations from underground reports written in the summer and autumn of 1941: "In a number of towns the local population carried out pogroms or even massacres of the Jews, unfortunately together with German soldiers"; "The entrance of German troops resulted in a vast terror against the Jews by the soldiers, unfortunately with significant participation of the local population." We read in these reports also about Poles assuming various posts in the auxiliary police and new local administration: "In smaller towns there is only *Hilfspolizei* composed of former Polish policemen and local Poles and Belorussians. . . . In town halls mainly the Poles are in charge"; "At the present time almost all administrative positions, except for the leading slots occupied by the Germans, are in Polish hands. . . . Some youth of fascist orientation and even members of former independence seeking organizations now serve the Germans and join militia units" (Machcewicz and Persak, *Wokół Jedwabnego*, 2:132, 143, 139, 147).

Jews.[81] Another organization, in which older Polish youth were compelled to serve by the Germans, the Baudienst ("construction work service"), was also used during the so-called *Aktionen*, when Jews were rounded up for deportation to death camps. Large numbers of Jews were murdered during roundups and embarkation on deportation trains, and young Poles were complicit in their deaths. The only objection that Kraków's archbishop Adam Sapieha ever voiced to the mass murder of Polish Jews was to request, in a letter to Governor Hans Frank (the titular head of German administration in the GG), that young Poles from the Baudienst not be used in the roundups of Jews. Another organization with Polish personnel that was frequently deployed for the task was the Voluntary Firemen.

Further to the east, in the Reichskommissariat Ukraine, in Belorussia, and in the Baltic countries, over 300,000 local men joined various police organizations.[82] They made up the bulk of security personnel behind the Eastern Front and were involved in the second wave of killings, when Jewish populations in previously established ghettos were murdered. Romanian authorities under Marshal Ion Antonescu organized deportations of Jews to Transistria, where tens of thousands perished, while the Romanian army units fighting alongside the Wehrmacht on the Eastern Front carried out massacres of Jews on its own, for example in Odessa. The roundup in Paris on July 16 and 17, 1942, when over 13,000 Jews were caught and imprisoned at the Velodrome d'Hiver in appalling

---

[81] Emmanuel Ringelblum, *Polish-Jewish Relations during the Second World War* (Jerusalem: Yad Vashem, 1974), 136.

[82] Martin Dean, *Collaboration in the Holocaust: Crimes of the Local Police in Belorussia and Ukraine, 1941–1944* (New York: St. Martin's Press, 2000), 60, 70.

conditions, was carried out by the French police. Captured Jews were then sent to Auschwitz, from which only a few hundred returned after the war. In the second half of 1944, when Hungary was occupied by German troops, local fascists from the Arrow-Cross movement took the reins of power and began murdering their Jewish fellow citizens. That summer, in a lightning-fast action coordinated by Adolf Eichmann's staff, 400,000 Hungarian Jews, rounded up by Hungarian gendarmerie, were deported to Auschwitz.

How many Jews in occupied Europe—out of the total 6 million that were murdered—were killed by the "locals"? Most probably historians would estimate that number at between one and one and a half million. How many Jews were killed by fellow citizens in the prewar territory of Poland? That number could run to several hundred thousand. And how many Jews were murdered by neighbors and fellow citizens in ethnically Polish territories? The topic is still being researched, but one would be safe estimating that the number runs into tens of thousands.[83] But to understand what happened we need to dwell less on numbers and more on specific episodes.

[83] See press interviews with Professors Barbara Engelking-Boni, Jan Grabowski, and Jacek Leociak and Drs. Dariusz Libionka and Alina Skibińska from the Holocaust Research Center of the Polish Academy of Sciences: Aleksandra Pawlicka, "Spójrzmy prawdzie w oczy" (Let's face the truth), *Wprost*, no. 1 (2011); Joanna Szczęsna, "Obrzeża Zagłady: Jak Polska długa i szeroka" (Periphery of the Holocaust, all over Poland), *Gazeta Wyborcza (Świąteczna)*, January 8, 2011; Michał Okoński, "Sny o Bezgrzesznej" (Dreams about Poland without sin), *Tygodnik Powszechny*, January 1, 2011; Piotr Zychowicz, "Chłopi mordowali Żydów z chciwości" (Peasants were killing Jews motivated by greed), *Rzeczpospolita*, January 12, 2011.

THE KIELCE REGION

Since 2001, when the story of the murder in Jedwabne was first fully debated in Poland, historians of the Holocaust have studied court cases prosecuted after the war on the basis of the August 31, 1944, decree of the Provisional Polish government, the so-called August cases.[84] Two historians, Alina Skibińska and Jakub Petelewicz, examined all the "August" cases in the Kielce voivodeship and found that they contained evidence for the murders of several hundred Jews by Poles in the countryside of this region. Altogether about 250 people were brought to justice there after the war for their alleged involvement. Skibińska and Petelewicz complemented their findings from archival sources with interviews they conducted in the area.

This source clearly reveals only the tip of the iceberg of the phenomenon under study—partly owing to a reluctance on the part of prosecutorial authorities to bring such cases to court after

---

[84] The decree provided for criminalization of broadly conceived aid and assistance furthering German occupiers' goals to the detriment of Polish society. Occasionally the murder of Jews was prosecuted under this law as well. Some two decades after the war, all the "August" cases from court districts around the country were conveniently assembled in one archival collection under the custody of the Main Commission for Investigation of Hitlerite Crimes. Today they are in the holdings of the Institute of National Memory.

For excellent examples of such studies, see Machcewicz and Persak, *Wokół Jedwabnego*, and the yearly publication *Zagłada Żydów: Studia i materiały* (Holocaust of the Jews: Studies and documents), published since 2005 by the Center for Holocaust Studies at the Institute of Philosophy and Sociology of the Polish Academy of Science, in Warsaw.

the war.[85] But most important, this is a body of evidence from which Jewish voices are almost entirely absent. These were not cases brought by Jews. The Jews who appear in these depositions had been killed. And there were no Jewish witnesses left to testify about the murders. This material, though affording us only partial insight, represents the *entirety* of an important collection of evidence bearing on the issue.[86]

We need to focus now on what is at stake here and what kind of question we are bringing to the evidence at our disposal. Essentially we want to decide which of the two interpretations of the phenomenon of murder and plunder of Jews by their fellow Polish citizens is more plausible. One interpretation would simply claim that "stuff happens" during war: people get killed; violence is all around and may get privatized at times; banditry is rampant;

---

[85] For a discussion of the rationale for adopting such a stance by the communist judiciary, see the interview with Judge Andrzej Rzepliński in *Gazeta Wyborcza* of July 19, 2002, and also his "Ten jest z ojczyzny mojej? Sprawy karne oskarżonych o wymordowanie Żydów w Jedwabnem w świetle zasady rzetelnego procesu" (Is he from my country? Prosecution of people indicted for murdering Jews in Jedwabne in the light of correct rules of criminal proceedings), in Machcewicz and Persak, *Wokół Jedwabnego*, 1:353–459. An English translation of Rzepliński's interview can be found in Polonsky and Michlic, *Neighbors Respond*.

[86] By itself this does not necessarily allow us to obtain a reliable general portrait of what happened; one would still have to know about the ecology of the crime to make sure that all murder episodes have not clustered in some small subregion of the area, for example, or if the entire region can be considered "typical" with respect to this kind of crime, and similar to the rest of Poland. To allay doubts on this last point, let me mention a recent study of another voivodeship, Rzeszowszczyzna, where murders of Jews by local Poles are documented in at least 110 locations: Dariusz Libionka, "Zagłada domu Trinczerów—refleksje historyka" (Destruction of the house of Trinczers—Reflections of a historian), *Znak*, no. 4 (2008): 150. In any case, with these caveats in mind, *taking all of the evidence of a particular kind under consideration* is always a good practice.

people lose their moral bearings; there is always "scum" in any society, and anyway one should not generalize on the basis of isolated cases—in short, this was deviant behavior. But perhaps it wasn't. And to test that interpretation we must read the content of the cases to learn what actually happened and make sense of it.

Here are extracts of the August cases compiled by Skibińska and Petelewicz, spliced together from their article to make a narrative, describing the murder of Jews hiding in the Kielce countryside by the Polish population:

Altogether, in cases discussed below, there were over 250 people whose cases were handled by the District and the Appellate Courts in Kielce. Several hundred Jews hiding in the countryside of the świętokrzyski region were killed by the accused. . . .

Killings by shooting, with an ax, or using a wooden pole . . . were accompanied by acts of physical and psychological cruelty towards Jews who had been caught: women were raped, people were beaten, pushed around, cursed at and verbally humiliated. The accused [i.e., the alleged perpetrators of crimes against the Jews] . . . were peasants, [Polish] dark-blue policemen from outposts closest to the site of murder, members of various guerilla organizations, who frequently were the very peasants living during the day in their villages, rather than staying in forest detachments. In very many cases [*w bardzo wielu sprawach*] the accused held some position or function in the local officialdom: village heads, deputy village heads, district heads, employees of district office, members and commanders of local fire brigades, members of village guard. They were, without exception, of Roman-Catholic denomination, grown-up men, in general without a prior criminal record. They had stable family life, wives, and children. Some of them were members of the Communist party (PPR), or worked in the People's Militia (the police force) after the war. By virtue of their functions at least a part of them belonged to the local elite in the countryside.

Women had often witnessed and observed what had happened. They belonged to passive crowds, which carried the killings through the agency of a few of their most active participants. . . . One could even venture a proposition, based on depositions from witnesses and the accused, that there were many active participants and observers in almost all of these crimes. As far as murders perpetrated in villages are concerned, we can even speak of an aggressive, criminal crowd, where a few people play an initiating and leading role, while everybody else, by witnessing their crimes, provide at the same time a background, and a "moral" alibi for the crime committed.

In a certain sense the entire village takes part in the crime, with a different degree of involvement or witnessing, and after the war the entire village keeps the events, which took place with its participation, in its collective unconscious. This anonymous crowd constitutes an extremely important element for the analysis of this phenomenon. Its presence diffuses responsibility for the crimes committed and in a certain sense, silently, gives permission to do what was done to the Jews.

[In numerous files] we read detailed descriptions of the crimes, during which victims and perpetrators talked to each other. Jews defended themselves, begged and appealed to the conscience and pity of the killers ("After this man was killed this little boy stood up and said to everybody present: 'Poles, spare my life, I am not guilty of anything, it is my misfortune that I am a Jew'"). They tried to bribe the perpetrators with what they still had and thus save their lives ("We were playing cards when somebody dropped in and said that a Jew had been caught. . . . I went out doors. In front of the house stood a group of people and Moshek begged to be let go. He was with his little son, and they cried. This little Jew said: 'give them boots, daddy, maybe they'll let us go'"). Crimes were perpetrated against individuals known, often by name, against neighbors, against local folks.

A special category of perpetrators were the functionaries of the [Polish] dark-blue police, in their majority pre-war employees of the state police. Policemen implicated in crimes against the Jews were heads of families, typically with several children at home. Their material status was usually rather good. In their actions against the Jewish population one can notice a large element of freedom and independence from superior German authority. In the cases at hand there was not a single instance in which apprehended Jews were escorted back to a ghetto or to a police station—which would also mean death for them. They are usually killed right away or in a neighboring forest, and local peasants are ordered to bury the corpses. . . .

The direct motive to commit the majority of murders and denunciations of Jews hiding in the countryside was the desire to plunder them, to take over their belongings, which were imagined to be considerable. This was a pernicious consequence of a stereotype about Jewish wealth. Peasants imagined that by killing these people, they would get hold of their riches. One should suppose that in a psychological sense the fact that Jews in hiding were paying for shelter and food, and often paying very high prices by local standards, reinforced the belief that they have lots of money, which can be taken from them with impunity. Indirectly, the same motif underlay murders of Jews who no longer could pay off those giving them shelter. . . . People were getting rid of them, just as they were getting rid of Jews who had witnessed crimes committed earlier.

In over a dozen closely researched cases there is mention of characteristic and telling facts which accompanied the crime. After having finished, peasants gathered in the apartment of one of the participants to drink vodka, as if to celebrate with a meal their joint deed, to divide the spoils, and probably also to decompress. . . . [According to] depositions of the accused Władysław Dusza: "After they were thrown into a ditch [and] their clothes were taken off . . . we went to the apartment of Pawlik Władysław, who invited us for supper and served us vodka." In the deposition of the accused Stawiarski [we read,] "After we drank vodka the mother of Józef Dusza announced, speaking to us, that she is planning a wedding for her son, she said so because the Jewesses were already delivered to the police station, and her son before taking them there, used to visit one of the Jewesses."

This summary of the August cases offers a composite image. Not all of the enumerated examples are found in every episode Skibińska and Petelewicz scrutinized; it is nevertheless abundantly clear that any idea that the behavior they described was merely deviant would stretch credulity beyond reason. It appears that the killing of Jews by peasants in the Kielce countryside was socially sanctioned in multiple ways. Regular members of the community took part in them, not miscreants or "marginal" people, who are easily identifiable in any rural or small-town society. Indeed the local elite's participation bestowed upon these crimes a kind of official imprimatur. Killings were carried out openly, often publicly, drawing crowds of onlookers.

The analogy that comes to mind is that of a lynching[87]—with one important difference, however. Rather than to punish a real or imagined individual transgression, the true purpose of lynching is to teach a subjugated underclass a lesson—to discipline and keep it in its place. Jews, on the other hand, were not being taught anything in either the mass or individual killings to which they were subjected. There weren't any other Jews "to behave" one way or another in the local community; there weren't supposed to be any left alive. Socially sanctioned acts of murderous violence in the Polish countryside were not applied as mechanisms of social control but as instruments of annihilation.

The perpetrators of these crimes, the most active participants, remained, as far as one can tell, members of local communities in good standing. (As was mentioned earlier, some

[87] That relaxed posture of people in the photograph also fits the analogy, reminding us of photographs that white folks might take at the site of a lynching. Polish peasants in the picture were not killing Jews at Treblinka, but merely profiting from the crime earlier committed there. But we also know that a number of Jews who fled after staging uprisings at Treblinka and Sobibór were later caught and murdered by peasants.

joined the Communist Party and the People's Militia after the war). In almost every file there are group affidavits signed by inhabitants of the village where murders took place, "vouching for the good and honorable character of the accused. This is proof," Skibińska and Petelewicz observe, "that the village was in solidarity with the accused and that in the consciousness of its inhabitants there was no need to prosecute or to expiate in any way for the crime."[88]

A close reading of Skibińska and Petelewicz's study makes us wonder whether asking how many Jews had been killed by the local population in Poland is the right question. Would finding an answer to it offer a proper measure of this most tragic aspect of Polish-Jewish relations during the war? Shouldn't we be asking, instead, how many murderers of Jews and their accomplices there were among the Poles? Because, to quote Scott Horton, an American legal scholar, "open criminality implicates all who know of the conduct and fail to act."[89] One Jew killed by one perpetrator—but in a public manner, with the approval and encouragement of a crowd of onlookers—represents a collective deed, implicating all those present, a group experience of ultimate transgression marking forever the local community where it took place, especially that people later had to live alongside the murderers. Isn't this why the memory of these crimes is passed in Polish villages from generation to generation?

[88] Alina Skibińska and Jakub Petelewicz, "Udział Polaków w zbrodniach na Żydach na prowincji regionu świętokrzyskiego" (Polish participation in crimes against Jews in the province of Świętokrzyski region), *Zagłada Żydów*, no. 1 (2005): 128.
[89] Scott Horton, "Justice after Bush: Prosecuting an Outlaw Administration," *Harper's*, December 20, 2008, 51.

"THICK DESCRIPTION"

Those detailed descriptions of crimes committed in the Kielce countryside provide an approach, a mode of analysis and presentation, that permits general insight into what happened. Both because events back then were so extreme and because we lack systematic data about the period, we need detailed knowledge about concrete episodes to reach this understanding.

Much of the evidence about killings or denunciations of Jews by peasants in the Polish countryside consists of uncorroborated personal testimony from survivors, their relatives, or acquaintances. Typically this testimony is brief and notes just the facts. Much of the time it is secondhand information—for example, sought out and acquired after the fact by a family member. Thus the body of evidence is not "systematic" in any sense of the word, and it has not been part of any "record." So, strictly speaking, we should abstain from generalizing solely on the basis of what we can find about the *frequency* and *distribution* of these crimes.

The frequency of these reports is sufficiently high and their distribution sufficiently broad, however, to preclude concluding that these were isolated episodes in strictly confined areas. But the heart of all this lies not in asking what percentage of Polish peasants were hunting down local Jews (we will never be able to provide reliable statistics on this), but rather how these murders were carried out. And, as a number of detailed narratives exhibit concurring characteristics, we can make a leap toward a general understanding of the phenomenon.

Such a leap is possible because a society with a common past and shared customs and institutions has a degree of internal coherence, analogous to a text or a system rather than to a quilt stitched together from randomly assembled pieces. As a result, practices and attitudes engaging its fundamental values (those concerning life and death, for example) must be intelligible beyond the confines of any single community. This is why, even in the absence of firm knowledge about the distribution and frequency of the murder of Jews by Polish peasants, we can still tell from close analysis of a discrete number of episodes whether such murders were an accepted social practice. Given the character of these murders—that they were done openly, were well attended, and were widely discussed public events—and given the fact that the people involved were regular people, including members of local elites, a "thick description" of localized community events yields knowledge about behavior in the peasant society at large.

CLOSE-UP OF A MURDER SCENE

In 1942 the village of Gniewczyna, located in another part of the country, had 5,000 inhabitants and was split administratively in two. In May of that year a group of local notables, including two village heads, a commander of the voluntary fire brigade, and half a dozen other associates, ferreted out several Jewish families hiding in the vicinity.[90] Men, women, and children—sixteen persons altogether—were brought to the house of the Trinczer family, centrally situated in the village, not far from the church. The Jews were held there for several days in two rooms separated by a small kitchen. One of the rooms was turned into a torture chamber. The women were raped there, while the men were subjected to water torture to make them reveal the whereabouts of goods (which they used to pay for food and shelter while in hiding) that they had stashed with friendly peasants. Once the torturers obtained the desired information, their emissaries visited those friendly peasant households, demanding the surrender of these "Jewish rags," lest the Gestapo be informed.

The word got around Gniewczyna that the Jews were being forced to give up what remained of their belongings. One of the Jewish women managed to run away from the torture house, but was caught by her pursuer, an acquaintance with whom she went to school, who dragged her by the hair back across the village. Her mother, who had avoided the dragnet, showed up the next morning kneeling on the steps to the church to beg the priest for the lives of her daughter and grandchildren. He declined to help.

. After a few days, when the torturers concluded that they had got all the Jewish property to be had, they called the gendarmes, who came to the village and were given a good meal. Then they took the Jews into the courtyard and ordered them one by one to lie face down on the ground. All of them, beginning with the small children, were shot dead.

---

[90] Tadeusz Markiel, "Zagłada domu Trinczerów" (Annihilation of the Trinczer household), *Znak*, no. 4 (2008): 119–146.

We owe this detailed description to an eyewitness, a boy of twelve at the time, who wrote the story recently—after, he says, all the main protagonists had died. But for this narrative, which appeared in the April 2008 issue of the Catholic monthly *Znak*, a historian's inquiry would have revealed only one mention of this mass murder in printed sources: a note in the registry of German crimes kept by the Main Commission for the Investigation of Hitlerite Crimes, stating that sixteen Jews were murdered in 1942 in the house of Leib Trinczer by gendarmes who came from a nearby town. That it was a crime for which local inhabitants were responsible, a well-known fact throughout the entire community, would not have been revealed to outside observers but for one man's personal testimony.[91]

The Gniewczyna murder scene foregrounds two phenomena, of which one is well known and the other is a speculation. Memory of wartime atrocities against the Jews is very well preserved (and passed on from generation to generation) in the Polish countryside. Journalists and scholars stumble upon it every time they take the trouble to make an inquiry. Reporters who went to Jedwabne early in 2000, before it became the site of a national scandal, got local people to speak openly about it. Ethnographic studies conducted in the countryside on other, related subjects—by Alina Cała in the 1980s and Joanna Tokarska-Bakir in 2006, for example—also revealed the same, almost inadvertent willingness to speak about

[91] Libionka, "Zagłada domu Trinczerów—refleksje historyka," 148. The Main Commission for Investigation of Hitlerite Crimes communiqué provides fourteen names of the victims, listing their age, including two one-year-old babies, as well as three- and ten-year-old children. Tadeusz Markiel and Alina Skibińska are planning to publish a larger study on killings of Jews in Gniewczyna and the vicinity.

the crimes.[92] The reason is that these occurrences were quite common, and therefore both quasi-normal and simultaneously rare events with "significance," and remained a subject of conversation at local gatherings for years to come.

The second significant aspect of the murder is the role torture played. Torture, it seems, was ubiquitous in peasant-Jewish encounters. One reads about the brutalization of Jews, including the rape of women, in numerous depositions. Peasant violence, killings, and rapes in the Kielce countryside, as we just read, were documented in those August cases prosecuted after the war. But the story of Polish-Jewish relations is hardly different when told by an ethnomusicologist who for dozens of years has been collecting peasant folklore and is enamored of Polish village life and its culture, and who has many friends there:

> The most painful thing for me is the attitude in the countryside towards Jews, and a universal sense of triumph because they are no longer there. Universal. And one more thing, which I rarely wrote about, and which weighs terribly on my conscience: the killings of Jews who were hiding in forests by the peasants. The number of these crimes and incidents that I know about it is a terrible burden. In the book I tell one horrifying story how the father of singer S. brutally killed two small Jewish girls, and how with his band he later raped and killed a Jewish woman hiding in a

---

[92] Alina Cała, *The Image of the Jew in Polish Folk Culture* (Jerusalem: Magna Press, Hebrew University, 1995); Joanna Tokarska-Bakir, *Legendy o krwi: Antropologia przesądu* (Legends about blood: Anthropology of prejudice) (Warsaw: WAB, 2008).

forest. And I also know a story, one of many, which I have not recounted, of how a beautiful young Jewess with two small children escaped from a transport near Białobrzegi. They knew her, everybody stressed this. She went into a forest and a bunch of young men her age, with wooden poles, followed her. She could have been 23 years old, the children were three and four. And some twenty youths beat them to death with those poles, just for pleasure, nobody got anything out of it.[93]

Historians as a rule have not paid much attention to such details, focusing on the fact of the murder instead. But when time and circumstances permitted, local people applied themselves to forcing the Jews to reveal where their mythical gold was hidden. Jan Grabowski recounts one such incident: "A certain Marian Haba sought shelter in Cholerzyn (a village not far away from today's Kraków international airport in Balice). He remained in hiding, in the village, until the locals heard a rumor that Haba had gold stashed in the area. A 'Blue' policeman summoned a while later by the peasants, said: 'When I arrived in the village, I saw not a human being but a shapeless form. People told me they had killed the Jew because he was said to have buried five kilograms of gold.'"[94]

---

[93] "Nikt mi nie przybył, z profesorem Andrzejem Bieńkowskim rozmawiają Małgorzata Borczak i Ewa Sławińska-Dahlig" (No one came: Małgorzata Borczak and Ewa Sławińska-Dahlig in conversation with Professor Andrzej Bieńkowski), *Nowe Książki*, no. 3 (2008): 9. Bieńkowski, a painter and a professor at the Academy of Art in Warsaw, is also an ethnomusicologist.

[94] Jan Grabowski, *Rescue for Money: Paid Helpers in Poland, 1939–1945*, Lectures and Papers Series (Jerusalem: Yad Vashem, 2008), 38.

We are slowly beginning to understand a disturbing feature that surfaces again and again in the way Jews collectively remember this period: a recurring observation that the "locals" (be they Ukrainians, Lithuanians, or Poles) were "worse than the Germans." Jews know better than anybody that the Holocaust was a Nazi invention, one that they carried around Europe as they conquered the continent. The disturbing feature in Jewish narratives of the wartime mentioned above can be explained by pointing out that death administered by people well known to the victims evoked special suffering, as they must have also felt betrayed.[95] But we now realize that death at the hands of neighbors must have been also, literally, very painful.

HUMAN AGENCY

What renders studying the Holocaust so frustrating is its facelessness: the unacceptable anonymity of victims unrecognized in their individuality at the moment of death, which every society marks with a solemn ritual, even for the lowliest and poorest. To invoke a million people gassed at Auschwitz, to paraphrase a well-known saying, is only to quote a number. But such is the nature of the subject and the evidence at our disposal that in writing Holocaust history references

[95] In another context the writer Gustaw Herling Grudziński, drawing on his experience in the Gulag, stated what is also at stake in our case: "There was something inhuman in this, something mercilessly breaking the only bond which seemed to naturally bind the prisoners: solidarity vis-à-vis the oppressors." *Inny świat: Zapiski sowieckie* (Another world: Soviet notes) (Warsaw: Czytelnik, 1991), 56.

to staggering numbers of victims cannot be avoided. Nonetheless we yearn to pierce the oblivion to which this relegates individual victims, if only because the violent death they suffered was by nature an intimate and personal experience. Restricted to abstraction, we would not understand what had happened, and our account of the Holocaust would not be truthful. Because, at the risk of stating the obvious, specific individuals were killed in this man-made calamity, and specific individuals carried out the killings.

Hence the power of photographs. They remind us most directly of human agency in what otherwise we would know only as a numerical phenomenon. Photographers literally put a face to people—sometimes victims and sometimes perpetrators.[96] The barely visible faces in our photograph may be of persons only marginally involved with Treblinka, possibly as traders on its outer perimeter during the war and later as gleaners. Unable to identify these people, we still seek out their faces in the photograph, as if by "reading" them one could gain some understanding. And it is at the periphery of the Holocaust that we come across the most abundant evidence personalizing what happened—when the killing of Jews were carried out by their Christian neighbors.

In a study about Eichmann and his men, an Austrian historian called his protagonists not bureaucrats but "pathfinders."[97] In fact this observation applies to all Nazi perpetrators in positions of authority over the Jews, as there was no ready blueprint, no bureaucratic routine

---

[96] Claude Lanzmann's *Shoah* was powerfully evocative by showing not only SS guards in conversation, but also "faceless bureaucrats" who made sure that Jewish victims were delivered to extermination camps in a timely manner.

[97] Hans Safrian, "Perpetrators and Agency: The Case of Eichmann and His Men," paper delivered at Workshop on Hitler's Europe: New Perspectives on Occupation, Wirtschafts Universitat, Vienna, November 9–10, 2009.

to latch on to, no standard against which to measure their performance, and everything was fluid in their enterprise. A felicitous phrase coined by Ian Kershaw to characterize the overall functioning of the Nazi system—that by following cues emanating from the top of the hierarchy rather than strict instructions, functionaries of the regime were "working towards the Fuhrer"—fits admirably as a description of the mechanism of the Final Solution.[98] No matter how large or small the domain over which they presided—a work detail, a barrack, a ghetto, or a camp—the men in charge of solving "the Jewish question" were improvisers. Raul Hilberg's painstaking reconstruction of bureaucratic coordination required to mobilize assorted resources of a modern state to kill millions of Jews cannot represent the entire process unless we realize that at the core of it lay improvisation. It is a point, incidentally, that Hilberg explicitly acknowledges in Claude Lanzmann's *Shoah*.

Of course, bureaucratic capacity as well as the advanced technology and scientific wherewithal of a modern state were necessary to carry out in a timely fashion the mass murder of millions of widely dispersed people. But bureaucratic apparatuses and bureaucratic routines are devised with specific goals in mind. And to apply them to different tasks requires adaptation and initiative. To put it in the simplest terms: the trains carrying Jews to death camps—again, so instructively discussed by Hilberg in *Shoah*—were not operating according to a regular schedule. These were specially chartered trains, and somebody had to request them and steer them through the maze of regular traffic to the terminus. They could have been ordered, or not; there could have been more

---

[98] In Ian Kershaw's, *Hitler 1889–1936: Hubris* (New York: Norton, 2000), chapter 13 is entitled "Working towards the Fuhrer."

or fewer of them; they could have moved faster or slower through regular traffic. And so it goes for virtually every aspect of the killing process.

At every stage of the Holocaust decisions had to be made. It is a phenomenon filled with individual initiatives, as the perpetrators were not simply cogs in a machine operating according to preordained rules. Far from it. What this means is that agency in the Shoah, to a degree we perhaps have not yet adequately recognized when thinking and writing about it, rests with a multitude of individuals. And there were, ipso facto, many chokepoints where their initiative could have been slowed down, temporarily halted, even derailed. This was a significant and viable alternative, because from a certain point on it was clear that the Nazis were going to lose the war. Consequently, to say that nothing could have been done once the Nazi policy of killing all the Jews had been set in motion is incorrect. Plenty of people could have done something, or, as it were, not done something. With the result that hundreds of thousands of Jewish lives could have been saved.

THE PERIPHERIES
OF THE HOLOCAUST

Our photograph evokes one more important overall characteristic of Jewish fate: that plunder as well as murder was a collective enterprise. Local people partook in it openly and in open cooperation, and crowds of gleaners scavenging through the ashes of Treblinka fit this mold very well.

Two broad categories of people were involved in exploitation of the Jews: those wearing uniforms and civilians. Uniformed representatives of the local population in occupied Poland, the so called dark-blue police, were made up for the most part from pre-war employees of the State Police (Policja Państwowa). In the photograph, taken shortly after the war, we see soldiers or po-licemen (the People's Militia, as the force was called then, pre-sumably to avoid the odium that the word "policemen" carried after the war). Some of them, quite likely, were recent anti-Nazi guerrillas who were eagerly recruited into the People's Militia.[99] Both the dark-blue police and the guerrilla units killed many Jews during the war, while the People's Militia had its own postwar record of violence against Jews.[100]

But as we consider the violence inflicted upon Jews by local people, both the number of murder victims as well as the value of plundered property amount to a small fraction of the violence inflicted on Jews by the Nazis. We must always remember that the catastrophe of European Jewry was caused by the Third Reich, which conquered most of the continent and eventually proceeded to murder all the Jews within its reach. All the interaction between the locals and the Jews, however violent, was but a supplement to—a small fraction of—the main disaster, which befell the Jews at the hands of the Germans. This book therefore pertains to what happened on the periphery of the Holocaust. But this periphery is

[99] Jan T. Gross, *Fear: Anti-Semitism in Poland after Auschwitz. An Essay in Historical Interpretation* (New York: Random House, 2006), 231, 232.
[100] Gross, *Fear*, chapters 2 and 3.

situated at a focal point of Jewish fate during the war, because the only way the Jews could have survived was with the assistance of the local population. Those who had no opportunity, means, or ability to engage with their non-Jewish surroundings were condemned to death—with the exception of a few thousand who miraculously survived in labor camps.

BACK TO PHOTOGRAPHY

With the invention of photography and its use in newspaper battlefield reports in the nineteenth century, the images and myths of war in general became de-heroicized. During the American Civil War, newspapers printed mostly lithographs, usually based on arranged photographs (photographic apparatus was bulky and cumbersome). The shocking character of these lithographs was offset by conventional rhetoric: the "fallen" were laid on the battlefield in an orderly way, their faces up. More often the image would show a battlefield after the bodies were removed. But photographs of the horrors of war were taken and leaked to the public. A breakthrough role was played by the photos from World War I, showing deformed bodies and mutilated soldiers' faces. They were widely reproduced by antiwar activists after that "war to end all wars."

Among the material proofs of the Shoah, a great importance is assigned to photographs, of which there are thousands. But there are many problems with their classification and understanding. Some of them were also staged, sometimes out of necessity. In a conversation with a historian from the Majdanek Museum, Krzysztof Tarkowski, Janina Struk learned that the famous photograph, supposedly made in 1944 and showing "820 thousands of shoes" that were believed to have belonged to those murdered in Majdanek, is in reality a composite of three separate photos. Tarkowski doubted that after the liberation there would be so many shoes in the camp, as the local population, continuously searching for jewels, pillaged most of them.[101]

The majority of the photographs of the Holocaust were, of course, taken by the perpetrators themselves. Each of these images shows only a single moment in the catastrophe: harassment, despoilment, killing. There are usually two sides shown in these photographs: those in power (soldiers, policemen, a laughing crowd) and those powerless (Jews, dead or alive). And although our photograph was taken after the war, it is a typical product of the Shoah. Its points of gravity are inert Jewish bones, and around these are people full of life and energy.[102]

---

[101] Janina Struk, *Photographing the Holocaust: Interpretations of the Evidence* (London: I. B. Tauris, 2007); see the Polish edition of the book, *Holocaust w fotografiach: Interpretacje dowodów*, trans. M. Antosiewicz (Warsaw: Prószyński i S-ka, 2007), 268.

[102] After the war still another kind of photography existed, in which Jewish bones and skulls were visible. Gabriel Finder and Judith Cohen called them photographs from the grave. These were the snapshots taken by the Jews returning to the towns and villages in search of the graves of their families, who would find, in the places of execution and in desecrated cemeteries, bones and skulls scattered around. Photographs thus taken in the "valleys of dry bones" were not destined for the public. This was private documentation taken usually right before emigrating. "They were taken by amateurs with no intention of reproducing or circulating them. They are simple, unalloyed pictorial statements from a liminal moment in the lives of most survivors: the moment between survival and departure" (Finder and Cohen, *"Memento Mori,"* 57).

In the iconography of wartime, a group of civilians in photographs most often represents victims. This is so especially when they are accompanied by uniformed men with weapons. Here, however, the civilians represent the perpetrators, though their activity consisted of digging and not killing. In another type of postwar photography, taken while the concentration camps were being liberated, the civilians (cadavers or sick prisoners) are extended on the ground, and those standing around them, in military uniforms, represent the liberators. Sometimes those who a few days before were also slotted to become cadavers are standing around, in their own uniforms: the striped camp outfits. But our photograph does not fit into this canon.

The skulls and bones neatly assembled in front in a row are an indication that this is a photograph in the genre of "trophy pictures." Like hunters who photograph themselves with the game they shot, Nazi murderers took photos of Jews at execution sites. German soldiers photographed themselves laughing heartily as terrified Jews cut each others' beards or performed other humiliating exercises.

We already know that Polish "dark-blue" police partook in the plunder and murder of Jews. The People's Militia is also on record bullying, robbing, and occasionally killing Jews in Poland after the war. Judging by the body language and mood of the people in our photograph, we are not witnessing a moment when civilians have been caught red-handed by the police. Were it to serve as evidence of criminal behavior the photograph would most likely show only civilians and a pile of human bones. Militiamen are in the photograph because they want to be there. The photo has been taken, in all likelihood, as a memento.

Those who took part in the implementation of the Holocaust— as evidenced both in iconography, or photographic documentation, and in memoirs, diaries, and historical narratives—are almost without exception male. Female perpetrators appear usually as camp guards (in camps for women prisoners), and mention of them is somehow particularly disturbing. And yet the Holocaust benefited people materially without distinction as to gender, age, or nationality. "In 1942," writes Saul Friedlander, "in Hamburg alone forty-five shiploads of goods looted from Dutch Jews arrived; they represented a net weight of 27,227 tons. Approximately 100,000 inhabitants acquired some of the stolen belongings at harbor auctions."[103] Between 1941 and 1945 there were almost daily auctions of Jewish property in Hamburg, and the city was not especially exceptional in this respect. The French priest Patrick Debois, while searching for mass graves of Jews in the Ukrainian countryside and talking to local witnesses, heard from one of his interlocutors, "One day we woke up in the village and we were all wearing Jews' clothes."[104] The same must have been true in numerous other localities east of the river Elbe.

What makes the Holocaust such an indigestible subject is precisely the fact of its *not* being a confrontation between narrowly defined protagonists. It is not a story that can be told by focusing exclusively on the Nazis (members of the SS and the Gestapo and ideological enthusiasts of the Third Reich) and the Jews. Ordinary Germans also participated in the Holocaust—state employees, the Wehrmacht, and the civilian population—by enjoying the fruits of the crime. The Holocaust is also a confrontation between institutions and civilian populations of occupied Europe and the Jews who had lived in these countries for generations.

---

[103] Friedlander, *The Years of Extermination*, 500.
[104] Father Patrick Debois, *The Holocaust by Bullets* (New York: Palgrave Macmillan, 2008), 97.

Similar to the photographs of Charles Graner, who captured scenes in Abu Ghraib that he felt were out of the ordinary, our photographer, also inadvertently, recorded the essence of what was going on.[105] The photograph conveys a deeper truth about the golden harvest made possible by the Nazi occupation of Europe. The local population living alongside the Jews for centuries by and large appreciated the Nazi policy of cleansing the area of Jews and figured out that it could enrich itself in the process.

Our photograph shows a situation that is post-, or even post-post-: after extermination and after plunder (at least temporarily). A line from a poem by Wisława Szymborska comes to mind: "after every war / someone has to tidy up."[106] The ground on the photo was first dug to bury the bodies, then was dug up again to pull the bodies out and burn them (when the camp was being closed and disguised as a field), and then was dug up again to find anything with exchange value. The ditches and pits in this photo are almost covered, probably only for a while. The earth will be disturbed again and again. The dead are not left to themselves; the gold seekers do not leave them in peace.

This is why this photograph is so shocking, although its shock is muffled by the effort of interpretation. It does not show murder, blood, death; we see skulls and bones picked clean but not as bright

---

[105] However, the picture on its own terms is misleading, because gleaners were not working the Treblinka necropolis as a team. Quite the opposite: they were afraid of each other, trying to keep secret what they found. This was not a traditional harvest, where a line of peasants yielding scythes moves together, in harmony, to cut down a field.

[106] Wisława Szymborska, "The End and the Beginning," in *View with a Grain of Sand, Selected Poems*, trans. S. Barańczak and C. Cavanagh (New York: Harcourt Brace, 1993), 178.

as the white peasant shirts and scarves. One has to understand where they come from, that they were dug out of this sandy, unquiet earth, dug out not long before, and most probably to be examined by plunderers, perhaps even by some of the very people in the photo. These strong, healthy-looking and lively people came from the environs; some of them are shoeless. Most probably they also witnessed the arrival and killing of those who were buried here, because they were living in the vicinity of this mill of death, the smell of which traveled over their houses and fields, and whose harvest they discover anew in the pits and ditches, in the piles of sandy ashes they were raking with sticks and shovels. The peasants from Treblinka are gazing at us, not at the bones. They are not looking as if to say "I have nothing to do with it," but to say "Nothing is going on." They look innocent.

CONVERSATIONS ABOUT JEWISH PROPERTY

In her memoirs, a prosperous miller's wife from Radziłów, Chaja Finkelsztajn, describes a scene at the same moment as the mass killing of Jews was unfolding in her native village on July 7, 1941. Someone approached her with a suggestion that she turn over what she owned, since she would certainly be killed together with her family. And it was only right, Chaja's interlocutor argued without malice, for the good people who knew the Finkelsztajns to get their possessions, or else the killers would be rewarded.[107] To a Jewish man trying to find a hiding place with a peasant acquaintance near Węgrów, the latter's son-in-law said matter-of-factly, "Since you are going to die anyway, why should someone else get your boots? Why not give them to me so I will remember you?"[108] Miriam Rosenkranz had a moment of déjà vu during the pogrom in Kielce: "The horror of the ghetto came back to me and this scene when I worked with plucking out [feathers] and we were about to go back to the ghetto, and they were saying that that's the end, that they were deporting us for sure; and then this [Polish] woman acquaintance looked at my feet [and the following exchange took place:] 'Really, you could leave me your boots, Missy.' 'But Mrs. Joseph, I am still alive.' 'Well, I wasn't saying anything, only that those are nice boots.'"[109]

What can historians do with this kind of evidence? Are these amusing anecdotes or rare insights into significant aspects of wartime reality? Whether we quoted three or thirty-three such conversations, we would still be confronted with a discrete number of episodes and remain, epistemologically, in the realm of anecdotal (as opposed to systematic) evidence. The answer to this dilemma is to keep asking *how* things were done in order to get a general understanding of *what* happened. And just as we could reach such an understanding by analyzing in detail the character of crimes committed, we can do likewise by learning to read people's

---

[107] Extensive excerpts of Chaja Finkelsztajn's memoirs are translated into Polish and printed in Machcewicz and Persak, *Wokół Jedwabnego*, 2:263–317. The episode is recounted on 305.

[108] Shraga Feivel Bielawski, *The Last Jew from Wegrow* (New York: Praeger, 1991), 72.

[109] *About Our House Which Was Devastated* [*Sefer Kielce*] (Tel Aviv: Kielce Societies in Israel and in the Diaspora, 1981), 200. While still alive Jews were treated as if they were temporary custodians of "post-Jewish" property.

minds, so to speak, wherever a record of conversations has been preserved.

Listening to these exchanges we are eavesdropping on truly extraordinary ideas, for these snippets of conversations are built on an inversion of essential principles regulating people's lives in common. The message, addressed to a Jew with the expectation of a voluntary surrender of property to a neighbor, is embedded and recast in an understanding of private property rights as well as the norm of good-will that should bind people living in close proximity. Until the time that these conversations took place, we could safely assume, local people viewed the right to private property as inviolable. The only occasion when they felt it might be suspended would be to relieve extreme hardship which befell other members of the community—as a result of fire, flood, or an earthquake—as an act of goodwill, sustaining reciprocity for times when extreme hardship would in turn fall on themselves. What does it mean that three different people on three different occasions (and one could, of course, quote many more similar exchanges, as they caught the attention of Jewish interlocutors and were recorded) express exactly the same, very unusual thought about matters of fundamental importance in the life of a community?

It is implausible that such convergence of ideas inverting the meaning of private property and neighborly obligation, as far as the Jews were concerned, was purely coincidental. Again we operate under the assumption that practices and important beliefs in society are interconnected and must be congruent. What is accepted as a matter of fact by one of its segments could not be directly negated by another, or else it would induce what psychologists call "cognitive dissonance." Thus we have to assume that this anecdotal evidence (and it would remain anecdotal even if we quoted ten or fifteen such episodes) is an indication of a shift in shared norms concerning acceptable behavior toward the Jews. To take Emanuel Ringelblum's formulation, it illustrates how the inhabitants of Polish towns and villages ceased to perceive their Jewish neighbors as human beings and began to treat them as if they were "the deceased on leave."

A CERTAIN KIND OF PATRIOTISM

It is important to develop ways of portraying the plundering of Jews for what it was: namely, a social practice rather than a criminal activity or the result of the deviant behavior of some rogue individuals. That that plundering was widespread and sanctioned is revealed precisely by the forms of reference to it captured in language.

We find an echo of this shift in expectations not only among individuals speaking about interpersonal relations, but in institutional opinions concerning relationships between groups, such as revealed in an early report of the underground sent to the London government in exile, indicating that Jews were nonresponsive to Polish (i.e., Catholic) fellow citizens' approaches to take their goods, even though it was clear that otherwise everything would only end up in German hands.[110] The author of the report seems

[110] "Frequently Jews prefer to have their goods confiscated by the Germans rather than to give them to Poles for use for some time." The quote is from an underground situation report for the period of October 15 through November 20 sent from occupied Poland to the government in exile in London, quoted by Dariusz Libionka, "'Kwestia żydowska' w Polsce w ocenie Delegatury Rządu RP i KG ZWZ-AK w latach 1942–1944"("The Jewish question" in Poland in the views of

to be saying that by not consenting to be despoiled by their neighbors Jews were favoring Germans over Poles. And so the stakes are rising: a recalcitrant Jew, unwilling to surrender his or her boots to a Polish acquaintance, is not only unfriendly, but, implicitly, also unpatriotic.

Conversely, when German decrees ordered Jewish commercial property and real estate into Aryan trusteeship—an opportunity for enrichment that was taken up with eagerness by Polish lawyers, for example—this was also defended by suggestions that trustees were rescuing this wealth from German hands. The main underground publication, *Biuletyn Informacyjny*, was not buying this line, as it warned the legal profession in an article on July 19, 1940, that such behavior was objectionable.[111]

Wartime plundering of Jews became a continent-wide affair. It took place from the Atlantic Ocean in the west to as far east as German armies reached in their campaign against the USSR, and was accompanied by opportunistic behavior of the local population (despite the locals also being subject to exploitation by Nazi conquerors). In a proclamation of June 9, 1944, to the people of Corfu signed jointly by the prefect, the mayor, and the chief of police, we read:

Government Delegate and headquarters of the Home Army in the years 1942–1944), paper presented at the conference Les Juifs et la Pologne, 1939–2004, January 13–15, 2005, Bibliothèque Nationale de France, Paris.

[111] For the best analysis of this phenomenon, see Jan Grabowski, "Polscy zarządcy powierniczy majątku żydowskiego: Zarys problematyki" (Polish trustees of Jewish property: An overview), *Zagłada Żydów*, no. 3 (2007): 253–260. For reference to the article in *Biuletyn Informacyjny*, see 259. It must be noted that *Biuletyn Informacyjny* was an exceptional publication, where not a single line with anti-Semitic overtones was published throughout the occupation.

As is also the case in the remainder of Greece, the Jews have been rounded up in the island of Corfu, and are waiting to be shipped off to labor camps. This measure is bound to be greeted with approval by the law-abiding native population of Corfu, and will also be of great benefit to our dear, beloved island.

Fellow Countrymen, Citizens of Corfu!

Now commerce is in our hands!

Now we will be the ones to reap the fruits of our labor!

Now food supplies and the economic situation will prove to be to our advantage, and ours alone!

Jewish property as a whole rightfully belongs to the Greek State and, as a result, to each and every one of us. It will be taken over and managed by the Prefecture.[112]

The sense of entitlement to Jewish property found different expression throughout Europe. In 1943 in occupied France, for example, in anticipation of German defeat, various associations were formed to protect the interests of those Frenchmen who had acquired Aryanized Jewish property. Such associations continued to exist, albeit under new names, after the liberation. They defended their constituencies fiercely against the restitution of Jewish businesses or apartments to their rightful owners. "Those who bought Jewish property protected French interests," one association argued. "By buying property that the Germans threatened to liquidate, the purchasers 'preserved a precious inheritance for the national economy.'"

---

[112] Original in the archives of the Museum of Greek Jews in Athens. We are grateful to Dr. Gabriella Etmektsoglou for sharing this document with us and translating it from the Greek.

Thus framed, stripping the Jews of their assets was cast as responsible and patriotic behavior. Little wonder that in April 1945 hundreds of demonstrators went to the streets of Paris crying, "Death to the Jews" and "France for the French."[113] As a rule the few Jews returning to their hometowns after the war—from Salonika to Paris, to Prague, or to Warsaw—were made unwelcome by former neighbors already comfortably ensconced in their old apartments and jobs.

HUNTING FOR JEWS

Taking over Jewish property during the war had many guises, and it also came about as a result of friendly transactions between people who knew each other well. Once they were no longer allowed by German law to own anything, Jews who could do so tried to leave some of their property for safekeeping with trusted Polish acquaintances. In numerous instances this proved to be their salvation, providing financial resources on which they could draw when later hiding on the Aryan side. But frequently Polish acquaintances broke their promises, refused to honor the agreement, kept the goods for themselves, and even denounced Jewish owners to the German police.

Emmanuel Ringelblum wrote on the subject shortly before his death at a hiding place in Warsaw in 1944:

---

[113] Maud S. Mandel, *In the Aftermath of Genocide: Armenians and Jews in Twentieth-Century France* (Durham, N.C.: Duke University Press, 2003), 58–59. See also Renee Poznanski, *Jews in France during World War II* (Hanover, N.H.: Brandeis University Press, 2001), 464–467.

One of the most important economic matters in the field of Polish-Jewish relations was the problem of Jewish possessions and goods left with Poles for safekeeping. This practice dated from before the formation of the Ghetto, and was prompted by constant searches made by the Germans in Jewish flats. Then the only resort was to hand over these belongings to Aryans for safekeeping. At this time it was done on a mass scale. Belongings were given for safekeeping to former clients, partners and to Christian acquaintances in general. Goods had to be given to Aryans for safekeeping because of several anti-Jewish decrees— registration of all textiles, leather goods, etc. In many cases, the Jews entered into partnership with the Christians, handing over their warehouses and stocks on condition that the Jew should be a partner in the business. It usually turned out very badly for the Jew. The war had demoralized people who had been honest and decent all their lives; now they appropriated the Jews' possessions unscrupulously, in most cases not wanting to share even part of them. The Jews were treated as "the deceased on leave" about to die sooner or later. . . . In an overwhelming majority of cases, perhaps 95 percent, neither goods nor personal belongings were returned. Stock explanations were usually given that the things had been taken away by the Germans, stolen, etc. These Jewish belongings more than once supplied a motive for blackmail and denunciation. In order to eliminate an unwanted claimant, someone would turn him over to the "competent authorities."[114]

[114] Ringelblum, *Polish-Jewish Relations during the Second World War*, 77, 78.

Unexpectedly, because he shies away from giving numerical estimates, Ringelblum quotes a figure: "perhaps 95 percent," he says. We needn't take it literally, of course, because social phenomena under occupation can rarely be quantified. But one must pay serious attention to this estimate, which comes from a professional historian who organized a research group, Oneg Shabbat, which systematically assembled data on the life and death of Polish Jews under the German occupation. He was extremely knowledgeable about his subject. The Ringelblum Archive deposited in the Jewish Historical Institute in Warsaw, an indispensable source for the study of the period, was his creation.[115] It was a common occurrence still after the war that Holocaust survivors would have to file suit in order to retrieve property that they had left for safekeeping with friends and acquaintances.[116]

But Jews were preyed upon in a much more direct fashion during the war as well. As we've documented throughout this book, they became, literally, like hunted animals in the Polish countryside, and peasants joined in "hunts for Jews," *Judenjagd*, organized all over the Generalgouvernement by the German authorities. Occasionally Polish "dark-blue" police set out to hunt for Jews on their own initiative.[117] Fajga Pfeffer recalled:

[115] An excellent biography of Emmanuel Ringelblum has been written by Samuel Kassow, *Who Will Write Our History? Emanuel Ringelblum, the Warsaw Ghetto, and the Oyneg Shabes Archive* (Bloomington: Indiana University Press, 2007).

[116] See Gross, *Fear*, 42, 43.

[117] Two comprehensive monographs on this phenomenon were published in Warsaw in February 2011: Barbara Engelking, *Jest taki piękny dzień . . . Losy Żydów szukających ratunku na wsi polskiej 1942–1945* (The day is so beautiful and sunny: The fate of Jews looking for help in the Polish countryside, 1942–1945) (Warsaw: Stowarzyszenie Centrum Badań nad Zagładą Żydów, 2011); Jan Grabowski,

Once when I was walking deep in the forest I stumbled upon 6 policemen. They asked if I knew where Jews are hiding. I answered that I ran away alone and I don't know where others are. Then they asked if I wanted to live, and that I should tell them where the others were. I replied that they did not give me life, and so they cannot take it away. I looked terrible. I was all dirty black. They asked if I want to eat. I said that they shouldn't worry about my food, because they are not my caretakers. Then they requested that I tell them where the Jews with gold are. I told them not to look for cursed Jewish gold, that they have enough gold themselves because they got dark soil and white bread, which are better than gold. They kept questioning me for half an hour, until shots rang out suddenly. Jews hidden in the forest fired to scare the police off, and they ran away and I also ran into the forest like an arrow. They turned around once after me, but gave up. Before I fled I also said that they shouldn't hunt Jews like animals, because the time will come when these souls will have to be paid for. . . . At this time there were many victims in the forest and hiding places where police, *Volksdeutsche*, and peasants tracked down the Jews.[118]

Participation of local people is a necessary condition to ensure the effectiveness of genocidal policies. Planned extermination of *all*

Judenjagd: Polowanie na Żydów 1942–1945. Studium dziejów jednego powiatu (Judenjagd: Hunting for Jews 1942–1945. Study of the history of one county) (Warsaw: Stowarzyszenie Centrum Badań nad Zagładą Żydów, 2011).
[118] ŻIH, 301/1356.

members of a given population category, be it Jews in the General-gouvernement or Tutsis in Rwanda, is impossible without the involvement of their neighbors, the only ones who know who is who in a local community. Outsiders can effectively kill all the Jews already assembled in a ghetto, but for the most part they would be clueless trying to identify whom to put there or those who were hiding on the so-called Aryan side.

We read about Judenjagd in Christopher Browning's book, in which he quotes recollections of German policemen, accounts of these hunts by surviving Jews, and accounts by Polish witnesses.[119] A small-town schoolteacher from Łuków was traveling on November 5, 1942, through the Siedliska village. "I went into a cooperative store," he wrote. "Peasants were buying scythes. The saleswoman says 'you'll need them for today's round-up.' What round-up, I ask. 'Of Jews.' 'And how much do you get for a caught Jew,' I asked. Embarrassed silence. So I went on, 'for Jesus Christ 30 silver coins were paid, you should request as much.' Nobody answered anything."[120] In actuality, as a reward for helping to catch hiding Jews,

[119] Christopher R. Browning, *Ordinary Men: Reserve Police Battalion 101 and the Final Solution in Poland* (New York: Penguin Books, 2001), 155–158.

[120] ŻIH, 302/30, deposition of Stanisław Zeminski. See also Jacek Andrzej Młynarczyk, "'Akcja Reinhard' w gettach prowincjonalnych dystryktu warszawskiego, 1942–1943" (Action Reinhard in provincial ghettos of the Warsaw district, 1942–1943), in *Prowincja noc: Życie i zagłada Żydów w dystrykcie warszawskim* (Night province: Life and extermination of Jews in the Warsaw district), ed. Barbara Engelking, Jacek Leociak, and Dariusz Libionka (Warsaw: IFiS PAN, 2007), 70, 71; Malgorzata Melchior, "Uciekinierzy z gett po 'stronie aryjskiej' na prowincji dystryktu warszawskiego—sposoby przetrwania" (Escapees from ghettos in the province of the Warsaw district—Method of survival on the Aryan side), in *Prowincja noc*, 367; Dariusz Libionka, "Polska konspiracja wobec eksterminacji Żydów w dystrykcie warszawskim" (Attitudes of the Polish underground

peasants might get a few pounds of sugar, some vodka, or, most often, their victims' clothes.

Occasionally the Polish underground press reported the atrocious behavior of local people benefiting from the misery of the Jews. In *Information Bulletin* dated November 13, 1942, there is one especially poignant article, entitled "Disgrace":

> From various localities, actually from all places where bestial murders of Jews had occurred, one hears that the Polish population participated in the plunder of victims of German killings alongside the Hitlerites. . . . It turns out that frequently "solid" citizens, "serious" farmers, participated in these criminal displays. . . . In some instances fights broke out between those human beasts who were awaiting their turn until miserable Jews get killed, so they could strip still warm bodies of their clothes and underwear. In a few cases, the cordon of Hitlerite murderers was broken, as people couldn't wait till the execution, and proceeded to undress Jews condemned to death while pulling from each other's hands pieces of clothing.[121]

A passage from Father Debois's book illustrates a similar level of contempt for Jewish tragedy. In his research on the killings of Jews

toward extermination of Jews in the Warsaw district), in *Prowincja noc*, 484. Ample information about the pillage and killing of hiding Jews by the local population can be found in the archives of the Jewish Historical Institute, especially in Collection of Individual Testimonies no. 301. See, for example, testimonies number 119, 228, 281, 327, 379, 554, 569, 1136, 1142, 1145, 1153, 1298, 1422, 1474, 1477, 1599, 1640, and many others.

[121] Libionka, "Polska konspiracja wobec eksterminacji Żydów," 458–459.

in the Ukraine, Debois cites a story about golden crowns being pulled out of the mouths of Jews waiting in line for execution.[122]

Where is the border between indifference and hostility? The quiet with which the people are looking at us in that photograph is startling. After all, they are sitting around human remains. The gesture that placed the skulls and bones and blessed them with a sign of the cross at the same time turned them into things. (It was not for the bones that they were looking in the piles of sand; it was for what had an exchange value.) We know such sequences of skulls; we have seen them in the photographs of the victims of Pol Pot in Cambodia. The orderly row of skulls can serve as a judicial proof, but not as an expression of compassion. Only an individual skull invokes an individual fate. One could address a monologue to it, as in *Hamlet*. The indifference of the sitters, their gaze turning away from what is placed (what they placed?) in front of them means *These are not our bones. The bones of our dead would not be treated that way; they would not be exposed in the sand, without cover. They would demand respect, dignity.* And dignity, first of all, means separation, individuation. The mass graves of the men and boys from Srebrenica were combed for bones, which over a period of years were pieced together to reconstitute person after person. No gesture, no gaze in this picture indicates a link between the dead and the living.

Of course, these bones come from a mass grave, from a necropolis,[123] from "the bottomless earth" that denies the individuality

---

[122] Debois, *Holocaust by Bullets*, 97. Friedlander writes about similar episodes in Belorussia, in *The Years of Extermination*, 362.

[123] This is what Bożena Shallcross calls these terrains, in *The Holocaust Object in Polish and Polish-Jewish Culture* (Bloomington: Indiana University Press, 2011).

of death. Mass killing despoils death of its solemn singularity. Moreover these bones are Jewish—bones left in the ground, hiding valuables that used to be linked to them. The indifference of those photographed comes from the lack of recognition of the death of which these bones are a sign. If these were their bones, their death would mean offering, sacrifice, martyrdom. But this death does not concern the onlookers. They placed the skulls as one arranges the harvest, as if they were pumpkins or watermelons.

JEWS AND OBJECTS

A person's irreducible subjectivity is a value in itself, and any instrumentalizing of a human being is an abuse. During World War II the dehumanization of Jews reached very far. Those who met Jews during the occupation (and even later, as our photograph attests) identified them with possessions. The attention and efforts of those surrounding them were concentrated on collecting, segregating, and profiting from the objects gained from the Jews. Even after their death, their places of rest (*sic!*) were desacralized by the group digging in search of objects throughout the area where victims of mass murder were buried.

What is described below happened in some degree in every place in Europe from which Jews were expelled to death camps. In Warsaw, however, this was an enterprise requiring a special amount of energy, because in the Great Action from July 22 to September 24, 1942, more than 250,000 people were sent to Treblinka. The accumulation, selection, and distribution of objects left by the expelled and murdered Jews took several months. This account is provided by a surviving member of the Jewish police from the Warsaw ghetto:

> The collection of objects from apartments was conducted systematically by houses, streets and neighborhoods. Separate groups [of Jewish workers] collected glass and china, separate chandeliers, separate clothes and personal underwear, paintings and light furniture, separate heavy furniture. In every warehouse only one kind of object was stored. Every warehouse had its own signboard, with a number and specification of the section it belonged to. . . .
>
> The collected objects were moved to the offices for the private use of German civilians. Although there were four thousand people working from morning till dusk on this assignment, a lot of "stealing" was going on by Aryans, sneaking across the walls by night. A great number of objects was smuggled out by work-gangs leaving for work on the Aryan side and was sold for pennies, because they did not cost them anything. And still Jewish apartments were full of objects and furniture.
>
> Almost any larger space within the ghetto was turned into a storehouse, greater spaces for furniture and machines, smaller for other objects. Two churches on the terrain of the ghetto were turned into storages of furniture. The same with the Nożyk synagogue and the Great Synagogue on Tłomacka Street and the Judaic Library which were turned into storehouses of furniture. Furniture for sale was sent to the synagogue on Tłomacka, which was

located on the Aryan side, and to the Judaic Library. Any Pole had a right to buy furniture. It was sold by piece or by the sets, or even wholesale the entire content of a full warehouse, the number of furniture pieces estimated approximately.

Jewish policemen were ordered by the Germans to work on this gargantuan task as well. "150 policemen went to the synagogue every day to work as porters. . . . The functionaries worked in two shifts, one week in police service, the next one in the synagogue on Tłomacka."[124]

The area of the ghetto no longer inhabited was guarded by the Germans and a residue of the Jewish police, which made the pillage more difficult, but did not stop it. The emptied Warsaw ghetto, though surrounded by a wall, was very large. Before the liquidation of the ghetto, Marysia Szpiro, as she put it, "was going with merchandise" to the Aryan side. After the Great Action, during which the majority of her family perished, she remained with her brother and sister on the Aryan side and continued to support herself by smuggling. She had what was called a "good [i.e., un-Jewish)] appearance."

When we were crossing to the ghetto, everybody was already killed, so the Poles would take from Jewish apartments clothes, everything they wanted. Germans also would drive in with their cars and would take away everything from Jewish homes. Life was difficult for us then so we too would slip in and take away clothes and later sell them, and thus had enough to live on and everything.

[124] ŻIH, 302/27, Samuel Puterman, functionary of the Ghetto Police.

Germans did not allow Poles to take things out but wanted to take everything themselves. We did not pay attention to them not giving permission. We were going there and did not pay attention to anything. When a German caught us, we would say that we were Polish. Poles, too, were not permitted to go there, but when a Pole was caught then either they would take away everything and order them to go home, or would let them take what they had, but told not to come again. When we were caught, we asked that they not take it away from us, and sometimes they would let us keep it, and sometimes took it away. We brought everything to this lady, and what she liked we had to give her for her daughter, because if we did not, she immediately would scream that we are at her house, and she is keeping us, and we do not want to give it to her. Willy-nilly we had to, because of what would happen if she kicked us out. At that time, we were at least well dressed. Dora and Blina [a sister and a friend of the author] had good coats and everything.

Once we left the apartment when it was very warm. We left in summer dresses with nothing on our legs. We left everything at that Polish woman's. We returned in the evening and this lady did not want to open the door for us. We started to knock louder, and she came to the door and told us to go to sleep somewhere else, because Mietek [a Jewish boy who lived there too] had not come home and might tell about us. So, willy-nilly, we had to go somewhere to stay overnight. We went to the top of this apartment building. It was cold but what were we to do? Early in the morning, when it was still dark, we came down and went on the street as usual. In the evening we come back and knocked, and she started to scream: "Jewesses, what do you want here, who knows you here?" We saw that it is bad so we moved slightly away. A while later, I came to the door and asked her to at least give me my shoes because I was barefoot, and she screamed "go away, because I will give you to the police, you Jewess." We left this house.[125]

One more scene from Warsaw dramatically illustrates the picture of Jews as carriers of objects that others peeled away from them. Toward the end of June 1943, somewhere in the ruins of the ghetto, a German patrol pulled twenty-some Jews out of a bunker. The scene was observed through binoculars by a group of Jews hiding on the higher floors of a nearby burned-out building. Those captured were ordered to bring out from the bunker all of their possessions and then to undress. A young woman who resisted was shot.

Four SS-men, who obviously had the right to perform inspections, ordered the victims to place their clothes three meters away and then bodily examined them. SS men were lifting women's breasts, looking inside their mouths, then inspected their sexual organs. They were putting their fingers into their colons groping them like good housewives at the market searching for a fatty goose for lard. Then they ordered them to jump up and kick their legs up (perhaps a hidden diamond would drop out?), to squat down, etc. Towards those who resisted they used a radical method— they beat them up till they bled. Everybody, women, children

[125] ŻIH, 302/89, Marysia Szpiro.

and men, were subjected to these unheard of inspections. As witnesses, there were the ruins, debris, empty streets, blood-stained stones of the pavement and we, the miserable accidental viewers. The SS-men jeered and enjoyed the sight of the inhuman sufferings of their victims. Then they embarked on a thorough search through billfolds, wallets and purses, and on meticulous inspection of the clothes.

In the meantime the people dragged out from the bunker and now totally naked were sitting under a wall.[126]

SCHMALTZOWANYE

We have already discussed "Jew-hunts" in the countryside. The bane of Jewish life on the Aryan side in the cities were the *schmalt-zowniks*, blackmailers who extorted money from Jews trying to avoid deportation to extermination camps.

Starting in mid-October 1941 Jews were not allowed, under the penalty of death, to dwell outside of the ghetto. Schmaltzowniks who caught Jews on the Aryan side would extort money for not revealing their whereabouts to the German police. This practice was designated in Polish by a new word, as if the term "blackmail" did not capture the full meaning of what schmaltzowniks were doing. Because of the size of the ghetto, as well as the large number of assimilated Jews who tried to hide under assumed identities on the Aryan side, Warsaw was

[126] ŻIH, 302/113, Leon Najberg.

particularly affected by this scourge. Among Jewish survivors who spent time on the Aryan side and later told their story, one seldom finds a person who had not been accosted by schmaltzowniks.[127]

Extortion by *schmaltzowniks* begins the moment the Jew crosses through the gates of the Ghetto, or rather while he is still inside the Ghetto gates, which are watched by swarms of *schmalt- zowniks*. Every Jew who leaves the Ghetto is prey for a *schmalt- zownik*. . . . The *schmaltzowniks* operate in every place where Jews have some contact with the Aryan side—at all the posts near the walls, at the exit gates, along the routes to the work posts, at the work posts, etc., in short, wherever Jews try to "break loose," to detach themselves from the work post and go to a flat on the Aryan side. The *schmaltzowniks* walk around in the streets stopping anyone who looks Semitic. They frequent public squares, especially the square near the Central Railway Station, cafes, and restaurants, and the hotels where Jews who were foreign citizens used to be interned. The *schmaltzowniks* operate in organized bands. . . . They are a real plague of locusts, descending in their hundreds and maybe even thou- sands on the Jews on the Aryan side and stripping them of their money and valuables and often of their clothing as well.[128]

During a postwar debate about the demoralization of Polish youth under the occupation, Irena Chmieleńska, who had been commissioned by the Polish underground during the war to make a study of Warsaw youth, wrote that one of the main "sources of

[127] Ringelblum, *Polish-Jewish Relations during the Second World War*, 123.
[128] Ringelblum, *Polish-Jewish Relations during the Second World War*, 123, 124.

demoralization of children in Warsaw, was the Jewish issue. . . . Boys, sometimes as young as six, and usually ten or thirteen years old spent entire nights watching by the ghetto walls in order to blackmail Jews who were trying to sneak out."[129] The openness of this activity, as well as its public and group character, was the most notable feature. Why was there no effective social pressure from ordinary passersby, or fear-inducing sanctions from the Polish underground, which would prevent people from openly breaching the unwritten patriotic code, requiring that one does not assist the occupier in persecution of fellow citizens?

> An even more dangerous plague for Jews on the Aryan side is constituted by bands of blackmailers. The difference between the *schmaltzowniks* and the blackmailers is that the former's area of activity is the street and the latter's is the flat. Through surveillance in the streets, in the cafes, and by collaborating with the *schmaltzowniks*, the blackmailers find their victims; they call on them in their flats together with agents and uniformed police. If the *schmaltzowniks* are wasps that sting their victims, the blackmailers are vultures that devour them.[130]

And so there were also blackmailers (a distinction introduced by Ringelblum, but in the language of the epoch, they were also called *schmaltzowniks*) who carefully tracked down their victims and operated in groups, striving to maximize their profits by

---

[129] Irena Chmielenska, "Dzieci wojenne" (Wartime children), *Kuz´nica*, December 9, 1945.

[130] Ringelblum, *Polish-Jewish Relations during the Second World War*, 126.

squeezing all of their money out of Jews in hiding. Jan Grabowski studied their methods on the basis of trial records found in German courts, where occasionally they faced prosecution—not because they had done harm to Jews but because German police fought corruption of the German occupation administration, and bands of extortionists often included German officials.

Contrary to postwar Polish historiography, it was not primarily "social outcasts" who blackmailed Jews, and "assumptions that criminals and repeated offenders predominate among *schmaltzowniks* are wrong," noted Grabowski. In the files of German courts that Grabowski studied, seventy-three accused in such trials "provided information about their background and education. And while a dozen or so belonged to criminal lumpenproletariat, among the others we find all the social categories: skilled workers, civil servants, artists, peasants, merchants, pastry cooks, four tramway employees, eight high-school students, one teacher of French. The blackmailer of the highest social standing was a young count who tried to extort money from two Jewish merchants."[131]

People also took to extorting money from Jews ad hoc, grabbing an opportunity when it presented itself. One young man, fresh out of high school, thus described his actions and motivation: "On the corner of Koszykowa and Mokotowska streets I bumped into two Jews unknown to me, and I decided to impersonate a Gestapo agent. My idea was to get some money from them, because I know that Jews always have a lot of money."[132]

---

[131] Jan Grabowski, *"Ja tego Żyda znam!" Szantażowanie Żydów w Warszawie, 1939–1943* ("I know this Jew!" Blackmailing Jews in Warsaw, 1939–1943) (Warsaw: IFiS PAN, 2004), 45, 47.

[132] Grabowski, *"Ja tego Żyda znam!,"* 32.

SHELTERING JEWS FOR PAYMENT

Sheltering Jews during the occupation could also be very lucrative. While the monthly cost of subletting a room during the occupation would run between 50 and 300 zlotys, depending on the period and the location, Jews in hiding had to pay as much as ten times more. They might even be charged such premium prices on a per-head basis when entire families were hiding together. And as they could not go out to buy provisions, their hosts made additional profit from selling them foodstuffs at inflated black-market prices.

That giving shelter to Jews could even be considered a business transaction immediately opens a series of questions. For example, what was the ratio between sheltering Jews as an act of humanitarian assistance and sheltering them because it was profitable? Though a specific answer to this question will elude us, it is clear from Jewish reminiscences that the "shelter in exchange for payment" arrangement was a common occurrence. Opinions widespread among Poles concurred; it was a consensus view that people sheltering Jews were getting rich as a result.[133] Those who sheltered Jews for humanitarian reasons (and thus would later be recognized by Israel as Righteous among Nations) routinely asked their wards at the time of liberation not to disclose that they had helped them.

---

[133] As expressed in the statement "It is obvious, that he who has money must be hiding Jews" (ŻIH, 301/196). Accordingly hiding Jews were frequently discovered because their hosts imprudently attracted neighbors' suspicion showing up in elegant clothes or, for instance, meeting their German imposed quotas for livestock or grain deliveries in a timely fashion. (Grabowski, *Rescue for Money*, 7).

Their fear, in part, was that they would be viewed in their own community as profiteers who had accumulated substantial wealth and consequently as prime targets for robbery.

When Jews in hiding were discovered by local people or a guerrilla detachment, the peasant household that gave them shelter would be pillaged "as punishment," on the principle that the family must have enriched itself with Jewish money. The Jews, as we already know from discussion of what happened in the Kielce countryside, would then be killed.

Offering shelter to Jews as a money-making activity undermines one of the axioms of postwar Polish historiography about Polish-Jewish relations during the war. It posits that a Pole caught hiding Jews would always be executed, together with the entire family. How, in such circumstances, could people even consider sheltering Jews as a means of making money? One can understand that some would take such a risk on principle, motivated by a belief that it was their moral and Christian obligation to assist a fellow human being in mortal danger, no matter what the consequences. But to put one's entire family at such a terrifying risk just to make a good profit?

Obviously people were not that mercenary. They acted on the basis of experience, which suggested that they were taking a calculated risk, which in their opinion must have been worthwhile. First of all, they knew—as we also know, having studied what happened in the Kielce region—that if caught hiding Jews, most likely Poles would not be killed. Indeed the likelihood of being killed in such circumstances was rather low. The reason—as everybody in the countryside very well knew—was that German gendarmes and policemen only rarely found hiding Jews, and did so usually by accident. Typically this might happen during a police action conducted for another reason altogether—in a search for illegally bred live-stock, for example, during an antipartisan action, a street roundup, or some other random circumstance. On the other hand, Polish intermediaries, such as the dark-blue police or neighbors who were very effective in tracking down hiding Jews, would usually deal with the matter without involving the Germans. A household would be pillaged as punishment, the Jews would be killed, and there the matter would end.

What further facilitated the decision to shelter Jews for money was the awareness that Jews can be thrown out at any time, or even murdered. Jan Grabowski gives many examples in his study on the subject, and quotes a telling statement from a Polish witness in a postwar trial: "He went to ask his uncle for advice what to do with the Jew. When he came back he said the uncle advised him to waste (*zmarnić*) the Jew."[134] Neither the uncle nor the nephew who participated in this exchange was a hardened criminal. These were times when a decision to "do away with a Jew" required from regular people at most a consultation with a family elder.

"After a few days, peasants Henek Chęć (commander of the fire brigade), Tomek Koper, and Bronek Boczkowski, after robbing them [Jews hidden in a barn] took them into a forest and killed them." To give another example, the forester Petelka "took the money and the goods [from Jews] and set the barn on fire," so that "mother, father, and grandpa were burned. He closed the barn shut."[135] Such examples can be found throughout documentation of the epoch.

---

[134] Grabowski, *Rescue for Money*, 34–37.
[135] ŻIH, 301/228, 301/305, statements by Chaim Grabel and Henia Rubinstein.

AN EXCEPTIONAL CASE

Before the war Baruch Elbinger was a textile merchant in Brzesk Nowy in the Kraków voivodeship. Of his family of five, he and two children survived the war. His youngest daughter perished after having been left with a Polish woman of their acquaintance, who after a couple of days chased the little girl out of her house. Toward the end of the war Elbinger's wife perished as well. But for more than two years the couple with their two children successfully hid with peasants. The family was lucky; the major part of it survived the occupation.

The history of the Elbingers illustrates the situation of coercion, of serial blackmail, to which the Jews who were paying for shelter were subjected. Although they had to behave as if their "keepers" were just partners in a transaction—shelter for money—Jews understood perfectly well that they were themselves only merchandise from which the other side wanted to profit as much as possible. (Of course, there were people who took in Jews for money and behaved honorably, with real compassion toward their forced tenants, but they were exceptions.)

The basic rule for Jews in these conditions was to parcel out one's possessions—household objects, clothes, or, if one owned them, merchandise, cash, or jewels—among a number of trusted people. The objective was to make it impossible for the host family to strip their Jewish tenants clean in a single swoop—an incentive to throw the Jews out of the house, denounce them to the police, or even murder them. The helpers had to remain convinced that only by keeping their wards could they make additional profits. As a result, Jews had to retrieve their financial resources periodically, either through intermediaries or in person. This exposed them to additional dangers, but the risks involved in contacts with the outside world seemed worth running.

The first peasant who took in the Elbingers did not at first want to say how much he would be charging. So they kept giving him "gifts" and payment in kind; as Elbinger put it, "The textiles were counted according to a low price." After three months he requested 1,200 zlotys a week, a gigantic sum. They were able to bargain it down to 3,500 zlotys per month. But the peasant continued to accept gifts. "The merchandise he took at almost 50 percent less, and when I proposed that he should assess them at normal prices, he screamed at me to give him knives and he would cut all of our throats."

Elbinger continues:

> For the next month, he agreed to 1,600 zlotys per month, with separate payments for food. For foodstuffs he took 100 percent more than their market value, and regarding the merchandise he wanted us to bring him, he demanded all we had, and said he would then keep us even after the war. In this way, he wanted to take away from us all we had and later destroy us, and this is what could be understood from his behavior. But for the moment we had nowhere else to go, so we had to promise that we would try to bring him what textiles we had left with other people. My wife, though it was dangerous for her, had to go out several or even more kilometers on the road in order to give them some textiles before the time specified; but to him this was not sufficient, because he was not getting at once all that we possessed. He started to

employ various torments. First, he stopped giving us bread. We decided to search for another hiding place.

In a neighboring village Elbinger's wife found a farmer who agreed to hide them, and they sneaked away from their original host. "In the second place," writes Elbinger, "our gehenna continued. We suffered, we were cold and hungry, and in addition they had a 17-year old son, who was a scoundrel, and often poisoned our life, tormenting our children in various ways. But when we complained to his mother, his mother scolded him and did not allow him to do it."

The Elbingers stayed for fifteen months with the second peasant. They learned that another Jew, named Grunbaum, was hiding in the neighborhood, and managed to meet with him. The Elbingers were hungry for news about family and friends, and also for a regular conversation with somebody who understood their situation. Their new acquaintance was hiding not far away, had lived in the country previously, and knew the local people. He sewed clothes for them and helped with work in the fields in exchange for food. Elbinger writes:

In the last months before Russians came in the peasants were saying that the bands of NSZ, AK and BCh [acronyms of various Polish anti-Nazi guerilla units] were searching for Jews and that when they found out where a Jewish family was staying, they shot and killed them. . . . I warned [Grunbaum] not to go out but only to sell what he could, to make a stock of food and remain in hiding. Also I said that because he had hidden his goods with peasants, and some did not want to give these back to him, they would strive to betray him and send him off from this world, or denounce him to a guerilla group that was looking for Jews to destroy.

I convinced him, and this is what he did. I also did not allow my wife to visit him, so as to better protect ourselves. But we were suffering terribly from cold, because my wife and two children and I were lying during this winter under one narrow quilt, and Grunbaum had only one child with him and had 2 quilts and promised to give us one. . . . We thought that the war would last through the winter. My wife decided to go one more time to get this quilt and later just stay in place and wait if possible for liberation. One morning early my wife went to Grunbaum and did not return.

Elbinger soon learned that his wife, along with Grunbaum and his seven-year-old son, were killed by a group of armed men at the house of the peasant where Grunbaum was hiding.

On the January 17, 1945, the Soviet offensive began and the Elbingers were liberated. "As for the possessions that we had been able to save before expulsion and divide between those of our acquaintances whom we considered better people, now after our return they didn't want to give them back. They said that Germans or Russians took them away, but the neighbors said that it was not true, because they did not see and did not hear about it. Three-fourths of our goods were taken by the locals. I with my children were now in a difficult and critical situation. Few of our relatives survived."[136]

[136] ŻIH, 302/68, statement by Baruch Elbinger.

Greed played a fundamental role as a motivation in the behavior toward the Jews during the occupation. But as Jan Grabowski writes:

An unusually important role in the process of the deletion [of Jews] was played by simple human envy. According to largely shared conviction the people who hid Jews were gaining a lot. This type of "unjust" enrichment was irritating to neighbors and acquaintances, who considered themselves as unjustly omitted in the redistribution of property that was happening in front of their eyes. Jewish property was becoming in this way "a common property," and the individual efforts to hide the Jews, a form of egoistical activity directed against the community. Often an argument was used that because German repressions can touch all of the local inhabitants, then there is no justification for profits to go to a few ones. It happened sometimes that in the villages groups of citizens would organize inspections where the people suspected of "Jewish sympathies" lived, or of those, who by their behavior (unexpected wealth, buying above means, etc.) attracted to themselves the attention of their neighbors.[137]

In the imagination of most Polish peasants, Jews equaled money. And since anyone who faced the danger of annihilation would pay to survive, the belief, however mistaken, became a foolproof formula, a self-fulfilling prophecy. This belief extended to Jews even after death, as demonstrated by our photograph.

[137] Jan Grabowski, "Ratowanie Żydów and pieniądze: Przemysł pomocy" (Saving Jews for money: The business of helping), Zagłada Żydów, no. 4 (2008): 89.

NEW RULES AND EXPERT'S
OPINIONS

During the war someone living in close proximity to the place where our photograph was taken offered an invaluable insight. We already have met him, the landowner from Ceranów, Józef Górski.[138] He was a patriot, an observant Catholic, and a well-educated supporter of the largest political party in prewar Poland, the National Democracy. Thus he was a solid citizen by any measure one may wish to apply. And he writes the following about the Holocaust in his memoirs:

> As a Christian I could not not feel compassion [double negative in the original] with my fellow human beings but as a Pole I looked at what was happening differently. . . . I considered Jews to be an internal enemy so I could not help feeling glad that we are getting rid of this enemy and, what's more, not with our own hands but thanks to the deeds of another, external, enemy. I could not hide satisfaction when I rode through our little towns, and saw that there were no more Jews. Asked by Thurm [a local German official with whom he was speaking on this occasion]: *Sehen die Polen die Befreiung vom den Juden als ein Segnen an?* [Do Poles perceive being liberated from the Jews as a blessing?] I replied *Gewiss* [Of course], sure that I was expressing the opinion of the overwhelming majority of my fellow nationals.[139]

---

[138] After the war, in Ceranów, a Soviet military airfield was established Soldiers who stationed there sometimes joined the diggers and used explosives to blow up large pits in the camp area in search for valuables.

[139] Górski, "Na przełomie dziejów," 288–291.

Górski had extensive knowledge about what happened in Treblinka and the vicinity. He knew about the mass murder of Jews, and the predatory behavior of the population in the surrounding areas. Getting the Polish countryside "rid of the Jews," of which he so heartily approves, was not an abstraction for him but a concrete reality affecting all the senses, just as the stench of burning bodies spread out from Treblinka for miles, carried in all directions by changing winds. And he didn't hesitate to state what he thought at the time and leave it for posterity in his memoirs.

In the matter of cleansing the fabric of Polish society of Jews, the *bien pensant*, university-educated landowner showed little compunction, though he witnessed the Holocaust in close proximity to an extermination camp. Should we be surprised, therefore, that inhabitants of thousands of small, isolated localities, dispersed all over Poland, gave a helping hand in the removal (and, in the last analysis, the destruction) of their Jewish neighbors—particularly when the whole machinery had been set up by somebody else and they were offered material incentives to join in the process?

Górski was reading the minds of his fellow nationals correctly. Some variation of the line "We'll have to put up a monument to Hitler for having gotten rid of the Jews" was overheard in private conversations all over Poland. We have testimony to this effect not only from Jews who were successfully "passing" as Aryans and later recounted what they saw and heard in their wartime milieus, but from numerous Polish witnesses as well.[140] Little wonder, therefore,

---

[140] As in this statement of the well-known conservative writer and publicist Józef Mackiewicz: "During the occupation one literally could not find a *single person* [author's emphasis] who hasn't heard: 'Hitler did one good thing by liquidating the Jews. But one shouldn't speak about it.' . . . Almost the entire nation was in agreement with this statement." Włodzimierz Bolecki, *Ptasznik z Wilna: O Józefie Mackiewiczu* (Birdlover from Wilno: About Józef Mackiewicz) (Kraków: Arcana, 2007), 660.

that when circumstances were right, a substantial number of people turned their thoughts and ideas into action.

Given such a consensus of opinion, it is not entirely surprising that highly placed functionaries of the Polish underground state advised the government in exile in London about a looming—what else?—"Jewish problem." The government's official position had been that all changes resulting from decisions taken by the occupiers involving geographical boundaries, citizenship rights and status, property confiscations—all purportedly legal changes, in other words—were null and void. But London was warned, repeatedly, from the home country that the matter was not as simple as it may have seemed. Return to the status quo ante and resumption by Jews of their economic role from before the war was an impossibility, reported Roman Knoll, the head of the Foreign Affairs Commission in the apparatus of the Government Delegate (the underground civilian administration in occupied Poland). The non-Jewish population had taken over Jewish positions in the social structure, he wrote in 1943, and this change was final and "permanent in character." He explained, "Should Jews attempt to return en masse [rumors and exaggerated estimates circulated about the numbers of Jews who had managed to escape into the Soviet interior and were expected to return to Poland after the war] people would not perceive this as a restoration but as an invasion, which they would resist even by physical means."[141]

In July 1945 another distinguished politician of the London-affiliated underground, Jerzy Braun, conveyed his observations about the growing anti-Semitism in Poland:

[141] Libionka, "'Kwestia żydowska' w Polsce."

Today there is no place for a Jew in small towns and villages. During the past six years (finally!) [emphasis in original] a Polish third estate has emerged which did not exist before. It completely took over trade, supplies, mediation, and local crafts in the provinces. . . . Those young peasant sons and former urban proletarians, who once worked for the Jews, are determined, persistent, greedy, deprived of all moral scruples in trade, and superior to Jews in courage, initiative, and flexibility. Those masses . . . will not relinquish what they have conquered. There is no force which could remove them.

It was understandable, he thought, that Jews who survived the onslaught but could not return to their hometowns might "leave ruined and broken telling the rest of the world that Poles are anti-Semites." But what they take for anti-Semitism, Braun concludes, "is only an economic law, which cannot be helped."[142]

Wartime reality eludes understanding when we set aside the ethical dimension of human behavior. Many important witnesses shared this awareness, as, for example, did Jan Karski, whom we quoted earlier. Another author of particularly insightful writings about the experience of war was an eminent scholar of Polish literature, Kazimierz Wyka. This is what he had to say in 1943 on issues brought up by Knoll and Braun in their memoranda:

The central psycho-economic fact of the German occupation will certainly remain the disappearance from commerce and

[142] Libionka, "'Kwestia żydowska' w Polsce."

services of millions of Jews [. . .and] an attempt to fill this emptied space automatically and by inertia by the Polish people. . . . Were the manner in which this elimination took place and the way our society desires to benefit from it acceptable on moral and factual grounds? Even if I were speaking only for myself and found no one who would back me up, I will repeat—no, a hundred times, no. The manner in which this has been done and the hopes it has generated are disgraceful, demoralizing, and base. The prevailing views on the moral and economic tragedy of the Jews held by average Poles can be summarized as follows: by murdering Jews Germans committed a crime. We wouldn't act this way. Germans have it on their conscience and they will be punished. But we—we have now only benefits to draw from what happened, and we will do so also in the future, without soiling our conscience, or bloodying our hands. It is hard to imagine a more abased form of morality than what our society demonstrates by thinking so. . . . The manner in which Germans exterminated the Jews is of course only their responsibility. *But our kind of reaction to this process falls on our conscience* [author's emphasis]. A golden tooth ripped from a corpse will be always bleeding, even if no one knew where it came from.[143]

And, truth be told, the population of Polish towns and villages got hold of Jewish property because Jews all over Europe, and ipso facto in Poland, were killed by the Germans. Some local

---

[143] Kazimierz Wyka, *Życie na niby* (As if life) (Kraków: Universitas, 2010), 291, 292, 293.

people seized the opportunity, while most observed what was going on and liked what happened. But though their involvement in these crimes was opportunistic, we must recognize that when such an opportunity arose, they were not shy about making use of it.

WHERE WAS THE CATHOLIC CHURCH?

Przemysław Czapliński, a Polish historian of literature, while writing about the iconography of the Jedwabne murders, made a startling discovery. He found an "unwitting implementation of a shockingly simple and expressive scenario, which was certainly not imposed by the Germans." In Jedwabne the Jews were forced to break into pieces the monument of Lenin built in the town by the Soviets, and to inter the stone fragments in a ceremony accompanied by the taunts of the surrounding crowd. Then the Jews were executed and their bodies were thrown into the same pit. Czapliński comments:

> The sequence of dragging Jews out of their houses, forcing them through the town streets, insulting them along the way, stoning them, humiliating them by forcing them to carry a monument, and finally, leading them to the barn spontaneously recapitulated the Way of the Cross. Thanks to the apparent automatism of this processional behavior, and also because of the search for the model for "the last way," the

adult community of Jedwabne reproduced the suffering of Christ. It is ironic that the Jews, whose persecution has always been justified by the long-ago killing of Christ, this time took on precisely the role of The Redeemer, with Poles filling all the roles customarily assigned to the Jewish characters. On that day, they were Judases who betrayed, they were the guards who placed the cross (here the monument of Lenin) on Christ's shoulders, and finally the executioners, who led Jesus to the place of torment. Because the script of the Way of the Cross had been set in motion, the inhabitants of Jedwabne, following the anti-Semitic interpretation of Christianity, not only knew how to act, but also were totally convinced that their behavior was justified.[144]

We could look at our photo as a religious image of suffering. The bones in the photograph are surrounded not only by a crowd of civilians but by people in uniform, reminding us of Roman legionnaires. There is also a halberdier, a militiaman, separated from the group, with his weapon placed like the spear that wounded Christ. The tormentors from Bełżec, Treblinka, and Sobibór used the name *Himmelweg*—"Way to Heaven" (and also *Schlauch*, i.e., "tube")—to denote the passages, hidden by branches and fenced by barbed wire, that linked the gas chambers with the barracks in which the Jews were ordered to undress. It was through these that

---

[144] Przemysław Czapliński, "Prześladowcy, pomocnicy, świadkowie: Zagłada i polska literatura późnej nowoczesności' (Persecutors, helpers, witnesses: Shoah and the Polish literature of late modernity), in *Zagłada: Współczesne problemy rozumienia i przedstawiania* (Shoah: Contemporary problems of understanding and representation), ed. Przemysław Czapliński and Ewa Domańska (Poznań: Wydawnictwo Zysk i S-ka, 2009), 160.

they were rushed to death. It was the Calvary, the Way of the Cross of the twentieth century.

But although religion is as important in the Polish community today as it was during the war, the Catholic Church is the Great Absentee in the story of the Shoah of the Polish Jews. The men and women in our photograph would go, dressed in their holiday best, to their church on Sundays, but there was little possibility that they would learn from the sermon the meaning of what happened in their parish—in the extermination camp. Jan Grabowski, having read materials from several hundred August cases, was astonished that the word "priest" does not appear there at all.[145] Another historian writes, "It is sad that the most important role in the conspiracy of silence and co-participation—by acquiescence—in these crimes, of course *sensu largo*, belongs to the Polish Church."[146]

Throughout the German occupation the Catholic Church was the most important Polish institution. To this day the parish priest remains the highest moral authority in Polish villages. And yet the documents from the epoch show no reaction by the Catholic priests to the crimes of genocide that were happening in exactly the places in which they were fulfilling their pastoral duties. Stanisław Ramotowski put a question to the parson from Radziłów: "'Does Father feel bothered when a murderer comes to the church in a fur taken from a Jew'"—"because everybody knew that Dziekoński is wearing Szlapak's fur." Father Dołęgowski "did not reply."[147] This

---

[145] Information from Professor Grabowski in a personal conversation.

[146] Krzysztof Jasiewicz, *Pierwsi po diable: Elity sowieckie w okupowanej Polsce, 1939–1941* (First after the devil: Soviet elites in occupied Poland, 1939–1941) (Warsaw: Oficyna Wydawnicza Rytm, 2001), 42.

[147] Bikont, *My z Jedwabnego*, 62.

question could have been posed to country priests in all the villages in which Jews lived before the war.

The case of Dziekoński was not isolated. "[Usually] peasants were wearing *spencerki*, short homemade jackets," said a baptized Jew who lived through the war in Russia and then returned to the Podlasie region, where he was treated as a non-Jew. "After the war, when somebody came to the church in a fur-lined coat, it was usually known that it was 'post-Jewish.'"[148] The words, quoted earlier, of the Ukrainian interlocutor of Father Debois—"One day we woke up in our town and we were all dressed in Jewish clothes"—can undoubtedly be applied also to many Polish towns and villages.

The Church's reckoning with the period of the occupation requires an explanation of why there was no reaction to the genocide that was being perpetrated before its eyes. Even Archbishop Adam Sapieha, especially respected for his defiant attitude toward the occupiers, did not protest against the Nazi murder of Jews to the head of the Generalgouvernement, Hans Frank. In any case, there is no known historical record of any such action on his part. In a book-length interview, Father Stanisław Musiał said that in Sapieha's pronouncements about the wartime fate of the Jews, as well as the pronouncements of other hierarchs of the Polish Church, there is "nothing, there is no trace of compassion or concern. This is terrifying."[149] A contemporary historian makes an even more

[148] Bikont, *My z Jedwabnego*, 73.

[149] Witold Bereś and Krzysztof Burnetko, *Duchowny niepokorny: Rozmowy z księdzem Stanisławem Musiałem* (A rebellious churchman: Conversations with Reverend Stanisław Musiał) (Warsaw: Świat Książki, 2006), 192. See also Leon Poliakov, "The Vatican and the Jewish Question," *Commentary*, November 1950, 442.

severe diagnosis. "In the documents of the period of 1942–1943 that are known to historians," writes Dariusz Libionka, "there is no trace of any sign of interest on the part of the bishops in the fate of Jews."[150]

In some tens of letters sent by the Polish bishops to Rome and published in the official Vatican selection of documents about World War II, *Actes et Documents du Saint Siège rélatifs à la Seconde Guerre Mondiale*, there is no mention of the extermination of Jews. Not even the situation of converts was broached, though it was a topic of concern on the part of the Catholic hierarchs from other occupied countries; they kept appealing, without success, to the Vatican for interventions in the converts' defense.[151] The most important and basically the only Church source of news from Poland about the tragic situation of the Jews is the letter sent to the Holy Seat by the metropolitan of the Greek Catholic Church, Andrei Sheptycky.[152] In contrast to the bishops of the Roman Catholic Church, he gave the order to hide Jews in the Greek Catholic monasteries and church buildings. (The hiding of Jews in Roman Catholic monasteries, where it occurred, was locally decided by individual church people.)

---

[150] The author continues: "No echo of the Shoah was heard during the third conference of the Episcopate called on June 1, 1943, i.e. some days after the quelling of the Warsaw Ghetto Insurrection." See Dariusz Libionka, "Polska hierarchia kościelna wobec eksterminacji Żydów—próba krytycznego ujęcia" (Polish Church hierarchy and the extermination of Jews: An attempt at critical appraisal), *Zagłada Żydów*, no. 5 (2009): 42, 43.

[151] Libionka, "Polska hierarchia kościelna wobec eksterminacji Żydów," 44, 45.

[152] We should add that the reply to the letter of Sheptycky, who wrote in it, among other matters, about the murdering of thousands of Jews in front of civilian population, does not mention this subject (Friedlander, *The Years of Extermination*, 464).

The Polish embassy in the Vatican was at the time delivering reports about the situation of the Polish population, the Church, and the extermination of Jews, and the main Church correspondent from Poland to the Vatican, Archbishop Sapieha, had to know about it. But, as Libionka stresses, this "knowledge of the diplomatic efforts of the government and the embassy did not release the Kraków archbishop from the duty to alarm the Pope about the tragic situation of the Church and of the Polish population." He goes on: "In relation to Jews, such duty was obviously not felt by Polish Church circles. Neither were there attempts to use the intermediary of the Polish underground or of private people, Italians or Poles, to convey to the Holy See some materials in this matter, even if only about the persecution of the converted."[153]

The unanimous silence of the Catholic clergy about the martyrdom of the Jewish nation did not stem from forgetfulness or vices of individual members of the clergy, some of whom behaved differently. It was a conscious attitude, a deliberate choice, based on a well-articulated worldview. A source authoritative in Church matters, repeating a prewar position propagated by the Church as well as others regarding the harmfulness of Jewish influences, was even able to consider as "a peculiar act of divine providence that the Germans, besides a multitude of wrongs they did commit and are still committing against our country, in this one matter gave a good opening in that they have shown a possibility of the liberation of the Polish society from the Jewish plague and marked out a way, on which we need to proceed, of course less cruelly and less brutally, but steadily. [For] it is a visible sign of God's will, that the

---

[153] Libionka, "Polska hierarchia kościelna wobec eksterminacji Żydów," 48, 49.

occupiers themselves contributed to the solution of this burning issue, because the Polish nation, soft and unsystematic, would never mobilize enough for the energetic steps that are indispensable in this matter"[154] This quotation comes from the *Church Report from Poland for June and First Half of July 1941* (*Sprawozdanie kościelne z Polski za czerwiec i połowę lipca 1941*). The report was prepared in Church circles in the summer of 1941. Most probably the news had therefore not yet reached the authors that here and there "the Polish nation" had been able to overcome its "softness" in its relation to its Jewish neighbors.[155]

Libionka concludes his study of the attitudes of the Church hierarchy with a chilling understatement: "Polish bishops had little to say about the extermination of the three million Polish Jews, whom they never considered co-citizens."[156] But when, after the war, a parish priest from the village of Jasienica finally said something, he not only did not condemn the actions of his fellow Poles toward Jews, but had this to say on the subject of digging in the

---

[154] Jasiewicz, *Pierwsi po diable*, 42, 43.

[155] In 2001 Krzysztof Jasiewicz wrote the following commentary on this text: "Opinions on the Jewish question expressed in this Church document—and this is an official document of the Polish Underground State, prepared in accordance with the office regulations and sent through the underground communication channels to the part of the Polish Government in London, written over a dozen days after the crime of Jedwabne—even if they are not truly representative, even if they were pronounced in a state of ignorance about this or that crime, require a public, very serious debate. And probably something more, something substantially more, especially because one cannot doubt that the author (authors) of this document knew well the situation that reigned at that time in the ghettos. And at that time that reality was already horrifying to anyone." Jasiewicz, *Pierwsi po diable*, 44. The full text of the document can be found in the appendix to Jasiewicz's book, 1195–1203.

[156] Libionka, "Polska hierarchia kościelna wobec eksterminacji Żydów," 69.

cemetery of ashes in neighboring Treblinka: "These are Jewish graves and golden laces or jewels should not remain in the ground."[157]

Wartime Church archives, despite repeated demands from historians, have been closed in all countries, including the Vatican. It is doubtful that Church-empowered custodians would keep them under lock and key if they expected that, when opened, they would improve historians' evaluation of the Church's attitude toward the Jews.

HYPOCRITE LECTEUR, MON SEMBLABLE, MON FRÈRE

So many incidents from this epoch seem in hindsight like bad dreams, or deeply disturbing hallucinations, or inventions of a sickened mind.[158] Consider the young shepherds who caught a boy in a meadow, pulled off his pants to check whether he was circumcised (i.e., Jewish), then debated whether to drown him right away or deliver him to the police.[159] Or the hamlet near Wadowice whose inhabitants collectively decided to chop off the heads of two Jewish children hiding in the village while they were asleep—and relented only after the woman who was taking care of the children put her little wards on a wagon and rode through the village pretending to

[157] Rusiniak, "Treblinka—Eldorado Podlasia?," 207.
[158] The title of this section is from Charles Baudelaire, *Les Fleurs du Mal*.
[159] Władyslaw Bartoszewski and Zofia Lewinówna, eds., *"Ten jest z Ojczyzny mojej"* (Kraków: Znak, 1969), 758–759.

take them away to drown them in a nearby river.[160] Or the public killings of Jews caught by peasants in the Kielce countryside. Or the young people in Warsaw during the ghetto uprising in the spring of 1943 who, when the Germans set the ghetto ablaze, gathered together to watch during their lunchtime break "how Jews are getting barbecued." Or the trusted men of the Church writing in an official underground report that it must have been an intervention of "Divine Providence" to bring Germany to cleanse Poland of its Jews. Or the astonishing statement that after the war monuments would be erected to Hitler for having liberated Poland from the Jews, which, instead of being the raving of a solitary madman, turns out to have been a staple phrase, repeated in some fashion all over Poland. Or the statement by Antosia Wyrzykowska (a deeply religious peasant woman from the vicinity of Jedwabne who gave shelter to seven Jews on her farm during the war), who told the journalist Anna Bikont that she would never reveal to a priest in Poland what she had done, and that her daughter was right to have thrown in the garbage Antosia's Righteous among Nations medal awarded by Yad Vashem, because she had no one to show it to anyway.[161] Or the people who were hiding Jews during the war extracting promises from those they saved never to speak about it to anyone, as they feared their neighbors' reaction.[162] Or the peasants from the Siedliska village buying scythes in a local cooperative to

---

[160] ŻIH, Kolekcja 301/579, statement by Karolcia Sapetowa.

[161] Bikont, *My z Jedwabnego*, 256.

[162] This situation continues to the present. In its March 6, 2010, issue, the most influential weekly magazine in Poland, *Polityka* (Politics), published an article by Cezary Łazarewicz titled "Righteous among the Nation": "501 Righteous, who saved Jews during the war are still living in Poland. Many of them until today are hiding from their neighbors in their own homes."

join in a "Jew hunt." Each of these stories seems like a nightmare, verging on absurdity, and yet we know that only a small fraction of such tales overcame oblivion and surfaced by some miracle to become public knowledge.

As we read documentation of the epoch the realization dawns on us that such statements and events, each of them at first sight shockingly improbable, add up to and cohere into a more general picture. And this compatibility and complementarity of thoughts expressed and situations encountered—judged at first as pathological exceptions to prevailing norms—suggest that they defined Polish interactions with Jews. We begin to understand that Jewish property became an object of desire well within reach of all, and that those who would not seize such an opportunity for enrichment were considered "incompetents";[163] that a person who killed or delivered Jews into German hands (which amounted to the same thing) remained afterward an accepted and often well-respected member of the local community; that the usual response of a Pole to Jews encountered on the Aryan side— always keeping in mind that most people during the war were preoccupied with their own affairs and therefore remained oblivious to the fate of strangers—was to unmask them rather than to offer them shelter.

[163] See, for example, the statement by the engineer Królikowski, who directed a construction project near Treblinka: "People were surprised that as a manager of a construction project who had a lot of cash at his disposal I did not get into trade, from which I could grow rich. Probably some thought I am a nincompoop, but I am proud that I came out from the vicinity of Treblinka hell with clean hands, my conscience unburdened by human suffering, with as little personal property as I had when I arrived" (Królikowski, *Wspomnienie z okolic Treblinki w czasie okupacji*, 29).

We will not find data to determine what percentage of the inhabitants of the Generalgouvernement gave shelter and assistance to the Jews; what percentage stood aside, oblivious to the Jews' fate; or what percentage participated in the pillage and killing. But as an epistemological foundation of our knowledge concerning what happened during the war, as an anchor to give us a solid understanding of the period, a lack of aggregate figures is compensated by the fact that a number of concrete episodes and situations (which, considered separately, may seem like outliers or impossibilities) provide a coherent portrait of the times.

Maria had to make a phone call. We entered a small pastry shop where she thought there was a telephone. As it turned out, there was not. Faced with this situation, Maria decided to leave me there alone for a few minutes, she bought me a pastry, choosing the least visible table in a fairly dark corner, and told me she would be back right away, as soon as she had made the phone call. She told the same thing to the woman who had served us, who must have been the shop owner. There were no more than five tables and very few people, I could hear everything. In the beginning, it seemed to me that all was calm, and I sat very quietly, like a mouse hiding beneath a broomstick, waiting as I'd been told to—and fortunately, nothing was happening. I ate my pastry, and what the women (there were no men) were chatting about among themselves didn't concern me. Yet after a while I couldn't escape the realization that the scene was playing out otherwise. It was difficult to harbor any doubts that I had become the center of attention. The women—perhaps shop assistants, perhaps customers—had gathered around the shop owner, whispering and observing me intently. By this time I was a sufficiently experienced Jewish child in hiding to understand at once what this meant and what it could foreshadow. My level of fear heightened radically.

. . . Fragments of their conversation reached me that were sufficiently telling. I was not experiencing delusions, they were talking about me. I would have most preferred to melt into the ground. I heard "A Jew, there's no question, a Jew.'" "She certainly isn't, but him—he's a Jew." "She's foisted him off onto us." The women deliberated: what should they do with me? . . . My situation was worsening from moment to moment. . . .

The women having discussed the matter and their curiosity now piqued, came nearer; they approached the table where I sat. So began the interrogation. First one of them asked my name. I had false papers, I'd learned my identity, and I answered politely. . . . Yet I heard not only the questions directed at me, but also the comments the women expressed more quietly, to the side, as if only to themselves, but in such a way that I couldn't fail to hear. Most often they spit out the threatening word "Jew," but also, most terrifyingly, they kept repeating, "We have to let the police know." I was aware that this was equivalent [to] a death sentence.[164]

The catastrophe of European Jewry came about because genocide, which in time became the cornerstone of Nazi occupation policies, was given a kind of consent, manifested in a variety of ways, by many societies, in countries that had been conquered. As

---

[164] Michał Głowiński, *The Black Seasons*, trans. Marci Shore (Evanston, Ill.: Northwestern University Press, 2005), 93–95.

Saul Friedlander has put it, "Not one social group, not one religious community, not one scholarly institution or professional association in Germany and throughout Europe declared its solidarity with the Jews (some of the Christian churches declared that converted Jews were part of the flock, up to a point); to the contrary, many social constituencies, many power groups were directly involved in the expropriation of the Jews and eager, be it out of greed, for their wholesale disappearance. Thus *Nazi and related anti-Jewish policies could unfold to their most extreme levels without the interference of any major countervailing interests* [author's emphasis]."[165]

And so the plunder of Jewish property became a common European experience. From the river Dnieper to the Channel, from Paris to Corfu, no social stratum could resist the temptation. And if one were to ask what a Swiss banker and a Polish peasant had in common (besides that each has an immortal soul), the answer, with only a little bit of exaggeration, could be a golden tooth ripped from the jaw of a Jewish corpse. As to the ladies who were in the coffee shop in Warsaw during the German occupation, where one day little Michał Głowiński tried to eat a cake—"normal, ordinary women, . . . hardworking, . . . religious, possessing a whole array of virtues"[166]—these are our aunts and grandmothers, *nos semblables*, who merely acted according to norms that were then in place.

---

[165] Friedlander, *The Years of Extermination*, xxi. Mark Mazower advances a similar but more general proposition on the overall character of European responses to Nazi policies of occupation: "For much of the war Europeans fell into line and contributed what [the Germans] demanded anyway. After 1945, this was conveniently forgotten." Mark Mazower, *Hitler's Empire: How the Nazis Ruled Europe* (New York: Penguin Press, 2008), 6.

[166] Głowiński, *The Black Seasons*, 95.

In the flow of stories we recorded in this book, we have sometimes mentioned other places and other peoples who were victims or perpetrators of similarly horrid events. Though reports of atrocities may be censored and self-censored, one stumbles upon them continuously. In Nicolas Werth's book about Soviet citizens deported to Siberia who in 1932–1933 were left on an island to starve to death, he quotes a woman describing her acquaintances "pulling gold teeth out of the corpses" and trading the gold in Tomsk for clothes and food.[167] Another writer, Józef Mackiewicz, records that in 1945 British soldiers by ruse and force herded Cossack officers into trucks to return them to the Soviets, condemning them to camps and death. This was accompanied by "trading": one cigarette for a watch.[168]

Such enumeration of atrocities does not lead to the generalization that everybody would do it, provided conditions were right. But nor does it permit a feeling of superiority. "Our moral problem with the Holocaust," wrote Yehuda Bauer, "is not that the perpetrators were inhuman but that they were human, just like ourselves."[169] That is why the photograph of Treblinka's peasants—also, undoubtedly, "normal, ordinary, hardworking, religious, and possessing a whole array of virtues"—in addition to evoking disgust, is so frightening: we cannot know for sure that it will not one day be pulled from our own family album.

---

[167] Nicolas Werth, *Cannibal Island: Death in a Siberian Gulag*, trans. Steven Rendall (Princeton, N.J.: Princeton University Press, 2007), xv–xvi.

[168] Józef Mackiewicz, "Zbrodnia w dolinie rzeki Drawy" (Crime in the valley of river Drawa), in *Fakty, przyroda, ludzie* (Facts, nature, people) (London: Kontra, 1984), 275.

[169] Quoted in Timothy Snyder, "What We Need to Know about the Holocaust," *New York Review of Books*, September 30, 2010, 80.

AFTERWORD

On May 5, 2006, a well-to-do gentlemen showed up in the small museum at the Bełżec extermination camp and handed the staff a golden ring. In an accompanying note he explained that he had been born in Bełżec immediately after the war. The family moved to a large city shortly thereafter. His grandparents remained in Bełżec, though, and he visited them as a child. "Everybody knew," as he put it, that Bełżec is a "gold mine." For his eighteenth birthday his grandmother gave him this golden ring.

It was a lady's ring, and so it remained in a box until 2005. It was summer, I was returning with my business partners from Berlin. We were driving in a fast car back to Szczecin. In the middle of our journey the driver, momentarily distracted, almost caused an accident at the speed of 200 kilometers per hour. In a fraction of a second—evidently it was fate—he managed to avoid colliding with another car. My life would have been cut short, but I was alive.

The following night I had a dream. It was very vivid. A young Jewish girl appeared and in a quiet voice she gave me an instruction. "Johnny" (that's how she was calling me,

Johnny), "you have my ring. Take it back to Bełżec and leave it there. It belongs to me."

This was a peaceful dream, as if an angel was talking to me. One usually forgets dreams, but this one is fixed in my memory forever.

It is May 5, 2006. I came from Szczecin to Bełżec to fulfill the request of the young Jewish girl from my dream. She had been cruelly deprived of her life. Why did she choose me? I feel better.

The ring and the letter are deposited now in the State Museum at Majdanek.

INDEX

Moscow, 46n78
Munich, 14
Musiał, Stanisław, 112

Napoleonic wars, 39
National Democratic Party
    (Poland), 32, 104
National-Socialism, 11, 17.
    See also Nazis.
Nazis, 3, 8, 18, 37, 46, 71, 72,
    112, 118
  Aryanization and, 12
  exploitation of conquered
    peoples, 78
  "forced sales" and, 41
  as inventors of Holocaust, 64
  occupation of Poland, 47
    (*see also*
    Generalgouvernement)
"Non Omnis Moriar" (poem),
    28n39
Nożyk Synagogue (Warsaw),
    88
NSZ (Polish guerilla unit), 101
Nuremberg rally, 17

Ogrodowczyk, Karol, 21
Odessa, 48
Oneg Shabbat, 82
Operation Reinhard, 4–5, 6–7

Paris, 48, 80, 121
partisans, 26n36
patriotism, 77–80
People's Militia, 52, 57, 68, 71
Petelewicz, Jakub, 50, 52, 56,
    57
photographs, 18, 65, 69–74
plunder. *See* looting.
Podlasie, 19, 26, 31, 33, 112
Poland, 7, 15–16, 68, 71, 117
  anticommunist
    underground, 26
  anti-Nazi underground,
    46–47, 77, 85, 93–94,
    106, 114
  division by Stalin and
    Hitler, 45–46
  government in exile, 77, 106,
    115n155
  non-Jewish citizens of as
    victims, 28
  profiteering, 37
  takeover of Jewish property
    in, 44, 108
police. *See* dark-blue police;
    Jewish police; *and*
    subentries under France
    and Germans.
Policja Państwowa (State
    Police), 68

Ringelblum, Emanuel, 47, 76, 80–82, 94

Romania, 16, 48

Rome, 113

Rosenberg, Alfred, 14

Rusiniak, Martyna, 23

Russia, Russians, 45, 47, 112. *See also* Soviet Union.

Rwanda, 84

Rzeszowszczyzna, 51n85

SA, 42n70

Sapieha, Adam, 48, 112, 114

Sakowicz, Kazimierz, 37

Salonika, 43, 80

San River, 45

schmaltzowanye, schmaltzowniks (blackmail, blackmailers), 29, 92–95

Schutzmanner, 47

Sereny, Gitta, 4

Shaulists, 37–38

sheltering for payment, 96–98, 99–102

Sheptycky, Andrei, 113

Shoah. *See* Holocaust.

Shoah (film), 65n96, 66

Siberia, Soviet deportations to, 122

Siedliska, 84, 117

Skibińska, Alina, 50, 52, 55–56, 57

skulls. *See* bones.

Slovak Jews, 4

Sobibór, 4, 20, 25, 31, 32, 110 uprising at, 56n87

Social Darwinism, 15

Sonderkommando (work units), 4

Sontag, Susan, 9

Soviet Union, 45, 46 deportations to Siberia, 122 German military campaign against, 78 in Jedwabne, 109 occupation of Poland, 47 *See also* Russia

Sprawozdanie kościelne z Polski za czerwiec i połowę lipca 1941 (Church report), 115

Srebrenica, 86

SS, 4, 6, 17, 18, 31, 65n96, 72 bodily searches of Jews, 91–92 Warsaw office of, 13n15

SS-Arbeitslager (Lublin), 6

Stalin, Joseph, 45, 46n78

Stangl, Franz, 4–5

Stary Miedzyrzecz, 38

state employment, Jewish
removal from, 15
State Police (Policja
Państwowa), 68
Stendhal (Marie-Henri
Beyle), 39
Struk, Janina, 70
szaber (appropriation), 29
Szczebrzeszyn, 42
Szczecin, 123–124
szmalcowniks. See
schmaltowanye,
schmaltzowniks.
Szymborska, Wisława, 73

Tarkowski, Krzysztof, 70
taxation laws, anti-Jewish, 11
Teeth, 13, 22, 29, 86, 108, 121,
122. *See also* gold.
Targówek, 36n62
thick description, 19, 58–59
Third Reich, 15, 26, 45,
68, 72. *See also*
Germany; Nazis.
Tłomacka Street Synagogue
(Warsaw), 88–89
Tokarska-Bakir, Joanna,
8, 61
Tomsk, 122
torture, 60, 62

trade, 37
between camp guards and
locals, 30, 31
between locals and newly
arrived prisoners,
34–35, 36
Transnistria, 48
transport to camps, 12
Trawniki, 31n46
Treblinka, 3, 4–5, 25, 26, 74,
87, 110, 122
make-up of personnel, 31
postwar activity at, 9,
20–23, 40, 68, 73n105,
104n138, 105, 115–116
preservation efforts at, 20
trading near, 30–31, 32–33,
65, 118n163
train station, 34, 35
uprising at, 56n87
trials (of camp guards), 20
Tutsis, 84

Ukraine, Ukrainians, 31,
32–33, 47, 64, 72, 86
underground, Polish, 46–47,
77, 85, 93–94, 106, 114.
See also partisans; Poland,
subentry Government in
exile.

United Nations, 8n7
USSR. *See* Soviet Union.

valuables, 10, 25, 31–33, 41, 87, 93. *See also* gold; household and personal goods; jewelry; money; possessions; precious stones and metals; property.
Vatican, 113, 114, 116
Velodrome d'Hiver (Paris), 48
Vienna, 6
Vilnius (Wilno), 26n36, 37
Vistula River, 46n78

Wachman, 31
Wadowice, 116
Warsaw, 13n15, 29, 32, 33, 34, 80, 121
   blackmail of Jews hiding in, 92–94

distribution of Jewish possessions, 87–92
ghetto uprising, 36, 117
postwar return of Jews, 80
Way of the Cross, 109, 111
Węgrów, 75
Wehrmacht, 48, 72
Werth, Nicolas, 122
Wilno (Vilnius), 26n36, 37
Witlich, 42n70
Wólka Okrąglik, 26n36, 33
World War I, 69
World War II, 39, 46n78, 87, 113
Wyka, Kazimierz, 107–108
Wyrzykowska, Antosia, 117

Yad Vashem, 117

Żłobek, 31n45, 32
Znak (Catholic monthly), 61
Zyklon-B (prussic acid), 14